Social Problems in India

Issues and Perspectives

Sunil K. Bhattacharyya

2021

Regency Publications

A Division of

Astral International Pvt. Ltd.

New Delhi – 110 002

First Published, 1994

ISBN 9788186030004 (HB)

Published by : **Regency Publications**

A Division of

Astral International Pvt. Ltd.

– ISO 9001:2015 Certified Company –

4736/23, Ansari Road, Darya Ganj

New Delhi-110 002

Ph. 011-43549197, 23278134

E-mail: info@astralint.com

Website: www.astralint.com

Dedicated to the hallowed memory of my elder brother Late Sailendra Chandra Bhattacharyya, an erudite scholar who left the land of living at the prime of his life.

FOREWORD

I have great pleasure in writing the foreword to the book of Dr. S.K. Bhattacharyya. This volume containing different articles on some important social problems bears the imprint of the author's inquisitive mind. His skillful handling of the subjects with a deep insight into a plethora of problems is indeed commendable. Through a brilliant analysis, he has brought into focus the enormity of the problems and the urgent need to find solutions.

The chapter-wise discussions on some specific problems with a clarity of ideas make the volume all the more interesting. The first chapter highlights the festering problem of crime with an analysis of its magnitude, the effectiveness of punishment and participation of people to tackle this problem. It has been thoroughly discussed with the help of various theories and factual statistics which reveal that the problem is fast rearing its ugly head in the country.

The second chapter deals with the problem of juvenile deviance, youth unrest and the generation gap. The unique feature of this chapter is a penetrating discussion on juvenile crime, its growing menace and measures to grapple with this problem through the implementation of the Juvenile Justice Act, 1986 which has come into force all over the country replacing the Children Acts of various States and the Central Children Act for the Union Territories. Moreover, the problem of youth unrest and reasons for the chasm between the young and the old have been explicitly elucidated by the author. While dwelling on the problems of the youth, the author has also made an attempt to draw attention to the problem of begging by children and suggested measures for its eradication. The author's anxiety to deal effectively with this problem is genuine and meaningful in the context of developmental activities in the country.

The third chapter throws light on the prevailing conditions of correctional services for adult offenders and the progress so far made in the implementation of the programmes of institutional and non-institutional treatment and training services. The author has rightly emphasised the importance of bringing about further improvement in the field of correctional services in the country so that incarcerated offenders, when released, may be rehabilitated back into society as decent citizens. Similarly, the fourth chapter is devoted to a detailed discussion on the plight of female offenders and efforts so far made to improve their conditions by providing more facilities in terms of separate institutions, training in useful crafts, adequate recreational facilities and after-care. The author has gone further to elaborate reasons for neglecting the treatment and training aspects of female offenders and put forward suggestions for amelioration of their conditions. The governmental efforts to improve their conditions by setting up commissions/committees have been discussed in detail and the possibility of success of such efforts indicated.

The fifth chapter focuses some alarming trends which have, of late, assumed considerable proportions endangering peace and tranquility in society. The author has lucidly dealt with the problems of corruption, terrorism, drug-abuse and gambling which present a grim scenario of the country. His analytical treatment of these topics is quite interesting, thought-provoking and awe-inspiring.

The last chapter brings out the hazards of the problem of population explosion in the country. The author has rightly pointed out some insurmountable difficulties in the wake of the increase in population and sounded a note of warning that unless timely action is taken to check the continuous growth of population in the country, it will spell disaster by the turn of the century and it will be well-nigh impossible to make a meaningful stride in respect of socio-economic progress. Side by side, other related problems like geriatric problems have been discussed at length and the author's critical views expressed in a convincing manner.

This book is a welcome addition to the literature on sociology including criminology, psychology and corrections. The significance of this book is that it will meet the critical need for anyone deeply interested in acquiring thoughtful and provocative viewpoints on various social problems. It will prove to be of great value to professionals in the field of social work and other related fields in general and students of sociology and criminology in particular who are interested in deep critical study of various facets of sociological problems.

(D. Pathak)
Former Chief Justice of
Guwahati High Court and of
Orissa High Court
Rehabari, Guwahati 781008

PREFACE

As usual, problems proliferate in a changing society and Herculean efforts are often required to stem the ominous tide of such problems. In India, there are innumerable social problems. Some of them have assumed alarming proportions and call for sustained efforts to find their solutions. Sporadic efforts so far made to deal with this adverse trend, have touched only the fringe. It has been amply realised that the people should be involved in a big way to make a united onslaught on the problems which have been defying solutions over the years. It is, therefore, essential to create awareness among the people as an important step so that all-round endeavour may be made to tackle them in the right earnest. In fact, the main problem is the problem of inertia, infinite patience and colossal ignorance of the masses. Their stoic indifference towards the mounting problems that have beset society and all segments of the people, has made the situation all the more deplorable.

I shall deem it a success if this book of mine generates an element of awareness among the people in general and the youth in particular. I am sure the articles covering various aspects of social problems will cater to the needs of the students of sociology, criminology and other social sciences.

I express my deep regards and grateful thanks to Justice D. Pathak, (Retd.), for writing an inspiring foreword to my book. My hearty thanks are also due to my friends and colleagues, particularly Shri Kaushalendra Kumar, Advocate, Supreme Court of India whose advice and encouragement immensely helped me in bringing out this treatise.

Some of the articles of this book were published in the Employment News. These have been reproduced here. I would also like to thank my sons Sayantan and Sandipan who ably assisted me in preparing the manuscript and comparing the proofs before publication.

160, Samaj Kalyan Apartments, Dr. Sunil Kanta Bhattacharyya
Vikaspuri,
New Delhi- 110 018.

CONTENTS

Chapter 1

CRIME

CRIME: ITS CAUSES AND REMEDIES

Since the dawn of human civilization, crime has been a baffling problem. Man's endeavours to fully grapple with it in order to end or arrest it, have proved partially successful. There is hardly any society which is not beset with the problem of crime. Violations of norms or rules do occur in a society, and has been aptly corroborated by Emile Durkheim in his esteemed treatise "*Crime as a Normal Phenomenon.*" He says: "A society composed of persons with angelic qualities would not be free from violations of the norms of that society. In fact, crime is a constant phenomenon changing with the social change."

In a society people have some norms, beliefs, customs and traditions which are implicitly accepted by its members as conducive to their well-being and healthy all-round development. Infringement of these cherished norms and customs is condemned as anti-social. Thus, many a writer has defined the term 'crime' as anti-social, immoral or sinful behaviour. However, according to the legal definition, crime is any form of conduct which is declared to be socially harmful in a state and as such forbidden by law under pain of some punishment. Paul W. Tappan has defined crime in his book "*Crime, Justice and Correction*" as "an intentional act or omission in violation of criminal law committed without defence or justification, and sanctioned by the law as felony or misdemeanour." According to another school of thought, crime is an act which a particular social group regards as sufficiently menacing to its fundamental interests, to justify formal reaction to restrain the violator. On the other hand, Raffaele Garofalo, an 'exponent of the Italian School of Criminological Thought' formulated his theory of natural crime, which meant the acts offending the basic moral sentiments of piety and probity. Similarly, Stephen has defined crime as an act which is both forbidden by law and revolting to the moral sentiments of the society.

Thus, the exponents of various schools of criminological thought have given their respective definitions of crime. But these definitions are not very clear-cut and free from confusion. It may, therefore, be pointed out that the criminal law gives a precise definition of forbidden acts that constitute crime and provides for the machinery and procedure to determine the violations and to identify offenders. Moreover, the criminal law establishes substantive norms of behaviour, and more clear-cut, specific and detailed standard than the norms in any other category of social controls.

The existence of crime in a society is a challenge to its members due to its deleterious effect on the ordered social growth. In fact, it leads to a colossal waste of human energy and an enormous economic loss. Therefore, in the days of yore, the only conception of punishment for crime was death or the infliction of physical pain. In the list of Roman penalties, there were death by hanging, hurling from the Tarpeian rock, crucifixion, beheading, drowning in the sack, exile or beating with rods. Besides these barbaric and arbitrary forms of punishment, prisons under the Roman Empire were also places for detaining offenders until they could be tried and executed. According to the reasoning of those days, a man who declared war upon society, forfeited his right to belong to it and as such he should be exterminated. As a result of the practice of such barbarous and inhuman torture and punishment, the Classical School represented by Beccaria and Jeremy Bentham came into existence. Beccaria was greatly influenced by the writings of Montesquieu, Hume, Bacon and Rousseau. His famous work "*Essays on Crimes and Punishments*" received wide acclaim all over Europe and gave a fillip to the criminological thinking in the contemporary west. He sought to humanise the criminal law by insisting on the natural rights of human beings. He raised his voice aganist severe punishment, torture and death penalty. On the whole, he was in favour of detecting the sources of crimes and wanted to ascertain why some categories of crimes were committed. These views of Beccaria were also supported by Voltaire and eventually resulted in the reduction of the rigours of the criminal law in a number of countries in Europe and abolition of capital punishment in a few of them.

Jeremy Bentham, the great English legal philosopher, was imbued with Beccaria's work and initiated penal reforms in England. He was like Beccaria an utilitarian and to him the only rational basis of law could be the greatest happiness of the greatest number. According to his principle of utilitarian hedonism, punishment should not be more than what is absolutely necessary to produce the desired effect on the criminal and society. He also recommended greater use of imprisonment as a means of punishment. Similarly, Samuel Romilly carried on the practical reform of the brutal criminal code of England with the help of James Mackintosh, Thomas Foxwell Buxton and Robert Peel. The early prison reformers like John Howard and Elizabeth Fry also made relentless efforts to bring about reforms in the penal system and emphasized special treatment of the criminal. In the U.S.A., the Criminal Code was humanised due to the movement of the Pennsylvania Quakers who were opposed to the imposition of corporal punishments prevalent during that period.

In an attempt to find a rational explanation of crime, a large number of theories have been propounded. Various factors like evil spirits, sin, disease, heredity, economic maladjustment, etc., have been put forward singly or together as leading to crime. With the advance of behavioural sciences, monogenetic explanation of human conduct is no longer valid. The latest trend is to adopt an eclectic view about the genesis of crime. However, some criminologists are still prone to lay greater emphasis on heredity and physical traits.

The first attempt to understand the personality of offenders in physical terms was made by Cesare Lombroso of the Italian School of Criminological Thought who is regarded as the originator of modern criminology. He was the first to employ scientific methods in explaining criminal behaviour and shifted the emphasis from crime to the criminal. His theory was that criminals were different physically from normal persons and possessed few physical characteristics of inferior animals. This atavism in the criminal is the portrayal of savage qualities of the remote ancestors of human beings. Lambroso termed the criminals with such atavistic qualities as 'born' criminals. This theory was carried forward by other criminologists like Enrico Ferri and Raffaele Garofalo of the same school. Lambroso's theory was, however, criticised by the modern criminologists for his anthropometric measurements on which he formulated his theory of criminal behaviour. Gabriel de Tarde, the French Jurist and social psychologist was the first criminologist to offer a social explanation of crime. According to him criminal behaviour is the result of a learning process. Just as a person picks up a trade in his childhood so also he learns criminal behaviour. It may also be mentioned that physiognomists had earlier made speculations regarding a direct relationship between the appearance and criminal propensities of human beings. Similarly, phrenologists also made an attempt to find meaningful correlation between the skull, the brain and the social behaviour of a person. These ideas have, however, fallen into disuse.

Social change, which is inevitable in a dynamic society, results in disharmony, conflict and cultural differentiation. On the whole, social disorganisation takes place and traditional patterns of social control mechanism totally break down. In the wake of such rapid social changes, the incidence of crime has gone up tremendously in urban areas, particularly in big cities. The rural migrants in new cities are unable to adjust to the impersonal heterogeneity of this formless mass of people. They are no longer controlled by the traditional norms and family loyalties. They become restless persons without associates. There is no sense of security. In the words of Durkheim, they become small particles in that world of "disorganised dust." Thus, the heterogeneity of the urban life destroys earlier congenial social relationships, creating a social vacuum which proves to be a fertile ground for criminality. Under such conditions, violence and crime proliferate.

Edwin H. Sutherland propounded a theory based on 'differential association' by which he had sought to explain that some techniques relating to the commission of crimes might be learnt through association with criminals and others were acquired in the normal course of education. He had further made it clear that what was actually needed to develop criminal behaviour was not the crime-committing technique but some sort of rationalisation to use the techniques for criminal purposes. This rationalising capacity is indeed learnt through the association with criminals. Sutherland's theory of differential association has been criticised on the ground that all those persons who came in contact with criminals do not become criminals themselves. Moreover, this theory does not adequately take into account the 'personality traits', 'personality factors' or 'psychological variables in criminal behaviour.'

Herman Mannheim has brought into focus the importance of economic factors in the causation of crime. According to him, poverty contributes both directly and indirectly to the commission of crime. However, poverty alone may not be a direct cause of all the economic crimes. Feeling of inadequacy, frustration and emotional insecurity often play a dominant role in giving rise to the criminal tendency. It may also be highlighted that a number of theories relating to the causation of crime are based on the Marxist Theory emphasizing that all human behaviour is determined by economic factors. Friedrich Engels corroborated this fact and attributed the increase in the incidence of crime in England during the period from 1815 to 1842 to the abject condition of the proletariat due to the class exploitation. William Aldrian Bonger also adopted the same approach in explaining the phenomenon of crime. He opined that the criminal was a product of the capitalistic system which created selfish tendencies. In such a system each person tries to get the maximum from others in return of the minimum from himself. Thus, Bonger identifies many evils in the capitalist system which are responsible for the spread of criminal behaviour. In fact, the theory of Radical Criminology is based on this concept and further explains that crime occurs due to the exploitation of the poor by the rich.

The importance of mass media in influencing the human mind has been repeatedly emphasized by some experts. Television and films can have the maximum impact on the viewers due to combined audio-visual impact. Most of the films shown either on T.V. or in cinema halls depict scenes of violence and what is worse, these are appreciated by young persons who often tend to imitate the same in real life situations. Juvenile delinquency is sometimes the result of what youngsters see in the movies and on television. Likewise, pornographic literature also has an unwholesome influence on the impressionable minds of the youth.

Some criminologists like Thorsten Sellin and W.C. Reckless have drawn attention to organised crime which is carried on as an illegal enterprise. According to Sellin, organised crime is "synonymous with economic enterprises organised for the purpose of conducting illegal activities and which, when they operate legitimate ventures, do so by illegal means." The goal of such activities is to amass huge profits through illegal means. The largest share of profits, however, goes to the manager and kingpin of the entire iniquitous enterprise, e.g., prostitution, smuggling, bootlegging, gambling, bookmaking, racketeering, etc. In the similar manner, Sutherland has explained his concept of "*White-Collar crime.*" It is different from ordinary crime as it is "committed by a person of respectability and high social status in the course of his occupation."

A white-collar criminal belongs to the upper socio-economic class who violates the criminal law while conducting his professional activities. Sutherland further points out white-collar crime is more dangerous to society than ordinary crimes because the financial loss to society from white-collar crime is greater than the financial loss from burglaries, robberies and larcenies committed by persons of the lower socio-economic class. In support of this contention, Marshall B. Clinard has brought to light how businessmen commit the wartime black market crimes by flouting the existing laws. According to him, the major types of black market activities consisted of overceiling price violations, evasive price violations, rationing violations, violations of rent ceilings, and record-keeping and reporting violations. Edelhertz also mentions a number of white-collar crimes, such as forgery, fraud, embezzlement by employees and illegal financial maneuvers by businessmen. The most dismal aspect in respect of these crimes is that there is no effective programme for the enforcement of the criminal law against them as white-collar crimes are committed generally by influential persons. They are able to resist efforts for law enforcement themselves.

The magnitude of the problem of various forms of crime in a particular country can be ascertained after an analysis of the criminal statistics. But the fact remains that these statistics deal mainly with recorded crimes. It is, therefore, not possible to detect all criminal acts committed by people in a country. In India, statistics available from "Crime in India," published by the

National Crime Records Bureau, Ministry of Home Affairs, Government of India reveal the incidence of total cognizable crimes under the Indian Penal Code and the local and special laws for the five years from 1987–1991:

Year	Crimes Under I.P.C.	Crimes Under Local and Special Laws	Total
1987	1406992	3589326	4996318
1988	1440356	3765669	5206025
1989	1529844	3847665	5377509
1990	1604449	3293563	4898012
1991	1678375	3370971	5049346

Although these statistics do not reflect the actual extent of crime in the country as a whole, distinct trends are easily discernible from them. It can be seen that there is a gradual increase in the incidence of crime in India. The more recent statistics* on crime indicates that the situation has further worsened. It is reported that there is at least one cognizable crime every seven seconds, one penal offence every 20 seconds, a property crime every minute, a theft every one and a half minute, a violent crime every two minutes, a burglary every four minutes, riots every five minutes, dacoity and robbery every 14 minutes, a murder every 15 minutes and a rape every 52 minutes. Moreover, 57414 crimes were committed against women during the year 1991 itself. It is, therefore, necessary to take appropriate measures for curbing crime and keeping it at a minimum.

For centuries, it was believed that crime could be controlled by inflicting severe punishment or penalties on the offender. So the object of punishment was vengeance, expiation, retribution, reparation for the harm inflicted, intimidation, satisfaction of the public conscience and the prevention of recidivism and new crimes. The idea gained ground in those days that the erring person would be made to realise his guilt, repent and pay for his crime so that others would refrain from committing crimes in future, and in this manner society would be best protected from the onslaught of the criminal, by a rigorous method of punishment and intimidation. However, in course of time, the futility of this approach and belief was realised.

*Source: Illustrated Weekly–26 December–1 January, 1993.

Recent developments in the field of psychology, sociology and criminology have opened up new vistas in comprehension of human behaviour. The conviction that man commits crime according to his free will is no longer valid. It has also been found that crime is a product of various factors and cannot always be explained on the basis of hedonistic calculations of pleasure and pain. It is, therefore, of utmost importance to do away with the system of barbarous punishments and make an attempt to curb and control criminogenic influences by adopting a sound correctional policy. This new thinking is based on the premise that, since crime is a social fact and human act, the process of dealing with a criminal does not come to an end after the offence has been legally defined and the penalty imposed on the offender in accordance with the law. It is also essential to understand crime as a social and individual phenomenon and the need to prevent its commission or repetition by adopting an attitude conducive to the resocialisation and reformation of the criminal.

In drawing up any programme for the prevention of crime and the treatment of offenders, it should be borne in mind that human nature is complex and it is not possible to comprehend it fully. It has, however, been realised that all human beings do not respond in the same manner to a given stimuli. Two individuals may commit the same crime, but each act differs from the other in its social, economic, psychological and environmental ramifications. This basic understanding has led to the innovation of a number of treatment methods for offenders. As a matter of fact, prisons are no longer regarded as mere custodial institutions. They have now acquired a new dimension as treatment and training centres for those who fall foul with laws. The emphasis has thus shifted from custody to training and re-education of offenders and from mere isolation to association of prisoners with the community. In course of time, it has been amply realised that protection of society can be better ensured if the offender is corrected and reformed through individualised treatment. At present, there are about 76 central prisons, 250 district prisons, 822 sub-jails, 27 open jails and 20 special jails for detention, treatment and training of prisoners in India. *However, the fact remains that prisons do not serve the purpose of training and rehabilitation of all categories of offenders. Imprisonment may

* Source: Report of the All India Committee on jail Reforms, 1980–83.

be appropriate to deal with certain categories of offenders, yet there are several others for whom prison sentence may produce deleterious effects, and instead of becoming useful citizens, they may become tough and frustrated individuals with an enhanced propensity for crime. Therefore, various non-institutional methods of treatment of offenders have been lately introduced, viz., probation, parole, premature release, community service, half-way houses, work-release, day-fine, etc.

Of all these non-institutional methods of treatment of offenders, probation is widely accepted as the most important correctional programme in the country. It has developed as an alternative to imprisonment. It aims at rehabilitation of offenders by returning them to society during a period of supervision rather than by sending them into the unnatural and socially unhealthy atmosphere of prisons. The offender is allowed to remain in the community and develop as a normal human being in his own natural surroundings. With the help of the advanced techniques of social case-work, the probation officer endeavours to bring about some change in the offender. At present, there are about 880 probation officers in India. In addition to probation, other community-based non-institutional treatment programmes are also in operation. In Britain, non-institutional services have developed tremendously as the judiciary itself had taken the initiative in the implementation of these programmes.

The objective of the institutional treatment is to correct the effects of the causative factors of criminality on the inmate in the controlled atmosphere of the prison, utilising the helpful factors in his personality, family situation and attitude. This approach helps the prisoner reconstruct his life-pattern with renewed vigour for adjustment to the socio-economic situations and healthy interpersonal relationships. This complex process of treatment covers four separate areas, i.e., medical and psychiatric, educational vocational training and correctional social work. During the incarceration, the prisoner loses contact with his relatives and friends. So it is of vital importance for the prisoner to maintain constant contact with the members of his family and others in the community and in this area of treatment, the welfare officer has a very important role to play. He deals with various problems of the prisoner that may stand in the way of his smooth rehabilitation and assists him in his overall planning at the pre-release stage.

The All India Seminar on Correctional Services held in 1969 deliberated on this aspect of the treatment programme in prisons and recommended that there should be at least one welfare officer for 200 prisoners in an institution.

It is also realised that mere treatment in institutions does not help in ultimate rehabilitation of offenders. It cannot bridge the gap between the institutional experience and the stigma society attaches to the released inmates. So the total punishment for crime never ends at the end of imprisonment. It continues as a life-long record and sometimes it becomes difficult for an offender to go back to the community as a decent citizen inspite of his sincere and genuine desire to live honestly. In many areas of community life a discharged prisoner finds himself handicapped and stigmatised. His problems are multifarious—psychological, social, economic, legal and the like. It is, therefore, of vital importance to develop after-care services as an essential requisite in the correctional field. An after-care organisation can extend help to discharged prisoners mainly in two areas, viz., (i) social rehabilitative services, and (ii) vocational rehabilitative services.

Under the social rehabilitative services programme, the after-care organisation can establish hostels for accommodation of discharged prisoners who are in need of such help. These hostels serve as half-way houses and help ex-prisoners adjust themselves to the outside world and get ready to face the reality. For want of proper organisation of after-care services at different places, many ex-prisoners cannot avail themselves of these facilities. Although there are some shelters and after-care hostels in some states, these institutions cannot even touch the fringe of this stupendous problem. To make the after-care programme effective, it is necessary to have legislation regulating the procedures of admission and duration of stay in the hostels for released prisoners. As things stand at present, discharged prisoners enter and leave after-care hostels at their sweet will. There is no legal provision to compel them to stay in the hostels for their benefit. On the contrary, some inmates of after-care hostels do not like to leave even after getting employment and other facilities. This situation creates problems for accommodation of new-comers.

In some countries like Britain, the after-care programme has been a good deal successful because prisoners are released from prisons on parole and licence and kept under supervision till the term of imprisonment expires. During this period, the released prisoner has to abide by the rules and regulations prescribed under the law. If such a system with necessary legislation is introduced in India, the after-care programme is likely to make much headway.

In the whole correctional process, there is need for effective control, supervision and assistance of the offender in the community. Efforts should be made to entrust the community with the responsibility of dealing with the problem of crime as the criminal is the product of the community and it is for the community to devise ways and means to solve this problem. With this end in view, it may be possible to establish at various levels, people's committees to tackle the problem of crime right from the apprehension of an offender to the final disposal of his case. The Nyaya Panchayat system representing community justice will be a welcome development in this sphere.

PUNISHMENT AS A DETERRENT

Punishment is a pain inflicted on a person for committing an offence. It is an unpleasant experience which is deliberately imposed by an authority upon a person for the violation of a law. Its main purpose is to dissuade him from doing what he intends to do. In other words, a person is prevented from perpetrating an anti-social act with a view to achieving social control. If we go through the history of crime and punishment, we come across harrowing tales of inhuman tortures inflicted on those who fell foul with laws. Thus, an offender used to be beaten mercilessly, dragged in the street, maimed and often done to death. The death penalty as the extreme punishment was regarded as the ultimate weapon to do away with the disturbing elements. It was carried out through fire, drowning, crucifixion, hanging, stoning, pushing down from a precipice, throwing in boiling oil, using sharp-edged weapons like sword, axe, breaking on the wheel, quartering by four horses, etc.,. In the Babylon of Haummurabi, in addition of fines, there were four forms of punishment, e.g., death, mutilation, branding and banishment. The techniques of execution were death by burning , drowning and impaling. On the whole, there were 37 specific offences which were punishable by death. Similarly, in England of 1780 there were approximately 350 capital offences. During the reign of Henry VIII, many thieves and vagrants were sent to the gallows.

The ultimate objective of such inhuman forms of punishment was that a person undergoing such inhuman tortures would realise his guilt, repent and never commit any anti-social act. Moreover, potential offenders would also refrain from doing any wrong in future. It was, therefore, deemed justified that punishment should be deterrent, retributive and exemplary. On the whole, an atmosphere of fear was sought to be created in the name of protection of society. In India also, the condition in respect of capital punishment was not at all congenial. Even during the reign of King Ashoka, the severity of punishment remained unchanged. According to the Manusmriti, cruel methods of punishment create terror in minds of people. The Mahabharata also contains identical views. The conversation between King Dyumatsena and his son Prince Satyavana reveals the rigid views of the King regarding capital punishment. Dyumatsena asserts, "If the sparing of those who should be killed, be virtuous and robbers be spared, all distinctions between virtue and vice will disappear." Thus, we find a plethora of such rigid views on the extreme punishment in ancient literature.

However, with the passage of time, various developments have taken place in the fields of criminology and other behavioural sciences. The age-old idea of severity of punishment for the purpose of protection of society has fallen into disuse. It has been amply realised now that fear is not the only factor that motivates a man. Love, loyalty, ambition, greed, lust, anger and resentment may lead a man to face even death by committing a crime. These apart, there is a special category of persons who are of unsound mind and cannot comprehend the results of their action. As a matter of fact, the guiding light that enables a man to distinguish right from wrong gets completely extinguished in such cases and punishment will have no value for this category of offenders.

In India, the Penal Code provides for the death penalty under sections 120(B), 121, 132, 194, 302, 303, 305, 307 and 396. Unlike the global trend, the death penalty has not been abolished in India. However, the legislative policy in respect of it has undergone a basic change. The old Code of Criminal Procedure, 1898 under section 367(5) provided that a person convicted for murder was to be sentenced to death as a normal rule and if a lesser sentence was intended, reasons were to be recorded in writing. Later on, by an amendment this provision was deleted and courts were free to award either death sentence or life imprisonment. Subsequently, the Code of Criminal Procedure, 1973 which came into force in 1974 provides for all such offences life imprisonment as a rule and death sentence as an exception. In suggesting the change, the Joint Committee of Parliament in its report had observed, "A sentence of death is the extreme penalty of law and it is fair that when a court awards that sentence in a case where the alternative sentence of imprisonment for life is also available, it should give special reasons in support of the sentence."

Accordingly, sub-section(3) of section 354 of the Code of Criminal Procedure, 1973 provides that "when the conviction is for an offence punishable with death or in the alternative, with imprisonment for life or imprisonment for a term of years, the judgment shall state the reasons for the sentence awarded and in case of the sentence of death, the special reasons for such sentence." As a safeguard against any arbitrary or summary trial in such cases, the Code of Criminal Procedure lays down an elaborate procedure regarding the imposition of death sentence. Inspite of the present liberal trend, the Law Commission in its 35th Report opined that 'having regard, however, to the conditions in India, the variety of the social upbringing of its inhabitants, to the disparity in the level of morality and education in the country, to the vastness of its area, to the diversity of its population and to the paramount need for maintaining law and order in the country at the present juncture, India cannot risk the experiment of abolition of capital punishment.'

While deciding the constitutional validity of the death penalty in the case of Bachan Singh V. State of Punjab (AIR 1980 SC. 898), the Supreme Court of India held, "The question whether or not death penalty serves any penological purpose is a difficult, complex and intractable issue. It has evoked strong divergent views. For the purpose of testing the constitutionality of the impugned provisions as to death penalty in section 302 of the Penal Code on the ground of reasonableness in the light of Articles 19 and 21 of the Constitution, it is not necessary to express any categorical opinion, one way or the other, as to which of the two antithetical views, held by the abolitionists and retentionists, is correct. It is sufficient to say that the very fact that persons of reason, learning and light are rationally and deeply divided in their opinion on this issue, is a ground among others, for rejecting the petitioner's argument that retention of death penalty in the impugned provision, is totally devoid of reason and purpose." The apex court went further to elucidate, "If notwithstanding the view of the abolitionists to the contrary, a very large segment of people, the world over, including sociologists, legislators, jurists, judges and administrators still firmly believe in the worth and necessity of capital punishment for the protection of society, if in the perspective of prevailing crime condition in India, contemporary public opinion channelized through the people's representatives in Parliament, has repeatedly in the last three decades, rejected all attempts, including the one made recently, to abolish or specifically restrict the area of death penalty, if death penalty is still a recognised legal sanction for murder or some types of murder in most of the civilised countries in the world, if the framers of the Indian Constitution were fully aware of the existence of death penalty as punishment for murder under the Indian Penal Code, if the 35th Report and subsequent Reports of the Law Commission suggesting retention of death penalty and recommending revision of the Criminal Procedure Code and the insertion of the new section 235(2) and 254(3) in that Code providing for pre-sentence hearing and sentencing procedure on conviction for murder and other capital offences were before the Parliament and presumably considered by it when in 1972-73 it took up revision of the Code of 1898 and replaced it by the Code of Criminal Procedure, 1973, it is not possible to hold that the provision of death penalty as an alternative punishment for murder, in section 302, Penal Code is unreasonable and not in the public interest."

In the Sixth United Nations Congress on the Prevention of Crime and the Treatment of offenders held at Caracas in 1980, the issue relating to the death penalty was discussed at length. While assessing the deterrent effect of the extreme penalty, the representatives of both the abolitionist and the retentionist countries forcefully presented their respective views. The Indian delegation, however, maintained that the issue whether the death penalty be retained or abolished, had to be decided in relation to the hard realities of the time and the socio-cultural conditions in a country.

In India, the corporal punishment of whipping was introduced by the Whipping Act of 1864 which was replaced by the Whipping Act, 1909. It was, however, abolished in 1955. In England, flogging was abolished earlier. In the U.S.A. also, whipping is no longer prevalent. Some studies conducted in the U.S.A. and England have revealed that whipping does not have any deterrent effect. Similarly, fine does not have any deterrent effect although in some cases the amount of fine is so excessive as to reduce the offender to poverty or in cases where the courts award imprisonment in default of fine. The family and dependents of the offender are hit by such punishments. But the fact remains that it is not exemplary as in its execution no spectacle is made.

Various theories have been adduced to explain punishment. In fact, punishment originated when the State took over the disciplinary power. It was introduced as a societal reaction to actions which, in accordance with the value system of society, are viewed as dangerous or harmful to society as a whole. According to Durkheim, crime is a violation of the collective conscience which consists of values held in common by the members of society. In some primitive societies, punishment for crime was rationalised in supernatural terms. Offensces were viewed as affronts to God or ancestral spirits and if violations were not appropriately dealt with, the entire community would incur their displeasure which would ultimately lead to its extermination. The common modes of punishment in such cases, e.g., sorcery, witchcraft, sacrilege, etc., were death and expulsion from the community. However, in course of time, the system of jurisprudence and the prevalent theory of punishment supporting the witch-trials and similar inhuman practices were assailed by some scholars.

Truly speaking, the middle of the 19th century ushered in an era of penal reform. Correctional thoughts took a new direction. It was a time when people were restless and wanted to know what produced social problems and how they might be alleviated. The doctrine of divine right could no longer influence the minds of people. Louis Philippe was dethroned and Ferdinand I of Austria also abdicated the same year. Ireland, Lombardy, Venice, Denmark and Schleswig-Holstein rose in revolt. Garibaldi unified Italy by revolt in 1860. Emperor Maximilian of Mexico was executed in 1867. In Japan, feudalism was abrogated and a constitution promulgated in 1889. These developments influenced the minds of men against social evils including slavery and this trend had its effect upon penological thoughts as well. The dignity of man and respect for his personality were highlighted during this period and in this yeasty atmosphere criminology and penology acquired new dimensions.

Cesare Bonesana Baccaria advocated a new idea. He published in Italy a treatise entitled "An Essay on Crimes and Punishments" which created a wide-spread sensation in the field of criminal justice. Other scholars like Voltaire in France were also impressed by the new idea. Beccaria had a positive philosophy and a detailed programme to replace the abuses of the old judicial system. According to him,the objective of punishment was not to exact vengeance but to deter the individual from committing crimes and this goal could be achieved by adjusting the degree of punishment to the severity of crime.

Cesare Lombroso of the Positive School of Criminological Thought has opined that a criminal act should be viewed as a natural event which is brought about by antecedent conditions. Hence, the age-old idea that a person commits a crime at his free will is no longer tenable and punishment is regarded as inappropriate and retributive. This theory is, however, confronted with some criticisms. It is argued that when punishment is intelligently applied, it can have constructive effects upon both the offender and the society. It is, therefore, a social necessity. Nevertheless, the Positive School of Thought emphasised that the purpose of criminal justice was to afford maximum protection or defence of society against the criminal. It recognised the value of individualised treatment for the criminal. In truth, it was this School of Thought which for the first time laid emphasis on the criminal rather than on crime. It was realised that the criminal and not the crime is to be punished and the punishment should be regulated solely by consideration of the prevention of crime and the treatment of offenders.

Imprisonment as a form of punishment was traditionally used for the custody of offenders. The main purpose was to deprive the offender of his liberty which is most precious to a human being. Soon after his admission into a prison, the prisoner is introduced to a new environment. His personal identity is completely lost. He is converted into a mere impersonal entity in a new social sub-group. Moreover, the effect of imrisonment of an offender is also damaging on his family relationship. Instead of reforming an offender, the prison often provides an ideal breeding ground for gambling and deviant sexual behaviour. The most serious thing which happens to a prisoner is the social stigma when he is released from the prison. He cannot be detained in the prison for all time to come. Sooner or later he has to go back to the community. He has to often face insurmountable difficulties in getting accepted by the community. People feel a sort of contempt for him. He becomes an outcast. In fact, his real punishment begins after the prison doors are flung open and he is thrown out. In such circumstances, an ex-prisoner does not hesitate to come back to the prison after committing crimes again. It becomes a vicious circle. Thus, imprisonment as a punishment at times leads to further crimes.

While dwelling on the problem of crime and punishment, it has been amply realised that all human beings do not respond to a given stimuli in the same manner. Two persons may commit the same crime, but each act differs from the other in its social, economic, psychological and environmental ramifications. This basic understanding has led to the innovation of a number of treatment methods for offenders. Consequently, prisons are no longer regarded as custodial institutions only but also as treatment and training centers for those who come into conflict with laws. Now the emphasis has shifted from custody to training and re-education of offenders and from mere isolation to association of prisoners with the community. It has also been perceived that society can better be protected from the depredations of offenders if they are corrected and reformed through individualised treatment. However, prisons do not serve the purpose of treatment and training of all categories of offenders. Therefore, in course of time, various non-institutional methods of treatment of offenders like probation, parole, premature release, community service, half-way houses, work release, day-fine, etc., have been introduced.

In India, efforts were made to introduce non-institutional services for treatment and training of offenders as far back as in 1850 when the Apprentices Act was passed. The Act provided that a child between the ages of 10 and 18 years who committed a petty offence, could be placed under the charge of a person capable of imparting him training in some crafts so that he might eke out a living on his own. The maximum period of apprenticeship for a boy was seven years. This was the first legislation in India emphasising the non-institutional treatment and training of offenders. Then the Reformatory Schools Act was passed in 1876. Under section 18 of that Act the Superintendent of a reformatory school might permit any youthful offender detained in such a school, to live under the charge of any trustworthy and responsible person or any officer of Government or a municipality, who was willing to receive and take charge of him.

Probation was first introduced in the Code of Criminal Procedure, 1898 as a non-institutional treatment method. In the field of correctional services, it is now widely accepted as a non-institutional programme of treatment of offenders. It has developed as an alternative to imprisonment. It aims at rehabilitation of offenders by returning them to society instead of sending them into the unnatural and socially unhealthy atmosphere of prisons. Thus, there is a growing realisation that prison sentence is not the best mode of treatment to ensure the protection of society. For many offenders incarceration produces deleterious effects and instead of becoming useful citizens, they may become tough and frustrated individuals with a propensity for committing further crimes.

In England also, a number of non-institutional methods of treatment of offenders have been introduced in pursuance of the recommendations of the Wooton Committee in 1970. Community service was one of the recommendations made by the Committee in an attempt to suggest a constructive alternative to imprisonment. Section 15 of the Criminal Justice Act, 1972 empowers the court to order offenders to perform unpaid work as a service to the community. The number of hours for which any such offender is required to perform work under a community service order shall be not less than 40 hours and not more than 240 hours. This scheme actually provides for an alternative to short term imprisonment. The man–power which is likely to be wasted in a gaol, may be harnessed both for the benefit of society and for the good of those who are incarcerated. This scheme goes to show that punishment can be constructive and the discipline of working regularly for the benefit of the community also serves as a deterrent.

From the foregoing discussions it transpires that imprisonment and other forms of punishment do not have sufficient deterrent effects and generally fail to achieve the ultimate objective of punishment, i.e., reformation and rehabilitation of offenders. A large number of prisoners are short-termers and for them, prison-sentence for a few months or a year does not help either the community or the prisoner himself. It is, therefore, necessary to implement non-institutional community-based programmes of treatment for offenders, particularly those committing trivial offences.

PUBLIC CO-OPERATION IN THE PREVENTION OF CRIME

The age-old idea was that an individual committed a crime of his own volition. Punishment should, therefore, be retributive, deterrent and exemplary. However, with the passage of time, the concept has undergone a qualitative change as the emphasis has shifted to correction, reformation and rehabilitation of the offender as a useful member of society. Achievement of this objective presages closer cooperation between the law enforcing agencies and the public. In fact, it has to be realised that the criminal is a product of the community and as such it is for the community to evolve a mechanism which will prevent generation of crime. Here lies the importance of public cooperation, and it has been rightly emphasised in the implementation of preventative and correctional programmes in the country. These programmes are mainly organised within the frame-work of prison legislation, Juvenile Justice Act, Probation of Offenders Act, Immoral Traffic (Prevention) Act, Anti-beggary Acts, etc., and implemented by the State Governments, and the union territories in their respective areas. All these Acts provide for utilisation of voluntary services of people in the community.

The first effort to enlist public cooperation in the implementation of correctional programmes was made through the Apprentices Act, 1850. It was an all-India legislation applicable to children in age-group of 10-18 years. It authorised magistrates to commit such children as apprentices to employers and provided for controlling the relations between them. Similarly, the Reformatory Schools Act, 1876, which was modified later in 189., provided that the Superintendent of a reformatory might, with the sanction of the committee of visitors, permit any youthful offender (inmate) who had attained the age of fourteen years, to live under the charge of any trustworthy and respectable person or any officer of government or a municipality, being an employer of labour and willing to receive and take charge of him on the condition that the employer would keep such youthful offenders employed in some trade, occupation or calling. The Code of Criminal Procedure 1898 contained provisions under Sections 42, 43, 44, 59 and 128 for public cooperation in respect of detention, apprehension and prosecution of offenders. These provisions have been retained under sections 37, 38, 39, 43 and 129(2) of the Code of Criminal Procedure, 1973 which came into force on April, 1, 1974. Section 37 provides that every person is bound to assist a magistrate or a police officer reasonably demanding his aid in (a) taking or preventing the escape of any other person whom such magistrate or public officer is authorised to arrest; or (b) the prevention or suppression of a breach of peace; (c) the prevention of any damage attempted to be done to any railway, canal, telegraph or public property. Similar provisions exist under sections 38, 39, 43 and 129(2) for enlisting public cooperation.

Moreover, section 17 of the Police Act, 1861 makes a provision for appointment of a public man as a special police officer. Private persons are also appointed as home guards and village guards and they are systematically trained to work as auxiliary police force, especially during emergencies. Truly speaking, people are the major reporters of crime, which triggers off the process of criminal justice in motion. The investigating police officer has also to assess whether the person involved in the crime is a casual offender and committed a crime due to his personal need or under the influence of an undesirable and unscrupulous person or he is a habitual and hardened criminal. While collecting the relevant information the police have to depend heavily on the public information sources.

The Juvenile Justice Act which has replaced the Children Acts all over the country provides that every juvenile court shall be assisted by a panel of two honorary social workers, possessing such qualifications as may be prescribed, of whom at least one shall be a woman. There is also provision for the recognition of institutions run by voluntary organisations which are found fit by the competent authority to receive and take care of a child entrusted to its care and protection on specified terms and conditions. At present, there are about 140 institutions run by voluntary organisations in various states and union territories to supplement the work of the official agencies. The voluntary organisations like Children's Aid Society, Indian Council of Child Welfare, Society for the Protection of Children, Guild of Service in India render welfare services to children including those falling within the purview of the Juvenile Justice Act. This Act contains elaborate procedures for active cooperation of voluntary workers and organisations in the implementation of the Act. It further provides for the constitution of an advisory board by the State government to advise it on matters relating to the establishment and maintenance of institutions, mobilisation of resources, provision of facilities for education, training and rehabilitation of neglected and delinquent juveniles and coordination among the various official and non-official agencies involved in the work. This board includes experts and representatives of voluntary organisations engaged in the correctional field. In addition to this, the State Government may renominate not more than three non-officials to be visitors for each of the institutions set up under the Act. Through their involvement in such bodies the people become conscious of their responsibilities for the reformation of the profligate youngsters and bringing them back to the community as law-abiding citizens.

There is a vast scope for associating people with the task of rehabilitation of young offenders in society. The Juvenile Justice Act has, therefore, emphasised the importance of after-care services and provided for organisation of such services by voluntary agencies for the purpose of enabling children discharged from institutions to lead an honest industrious and useful life. This Act further provides that voluntary after-care organisations have to maintain the minimum standards of services as prescribed under the Rules. This provision will not only help in improving after-care services rendered by voluntary organisations but also bring about uniformity in the implementation of the after-care programme all over the country. The Draft United Nations Standard Minimum Rules for the Administration of Juvenile Justice which were presented to the Seventh UN Congress on the Prevention of Crime and the Treatment of Offenders provide inter alia that voluntary organisations, local institutions and other community resources should be called upon to contribute effectively to the rehabilitation of the juvenile in a community setting and as far as possible within the family unit.

In the field of prison administration, the reformation and rehabilitation of prisoners are of paramount importance. All efforts are made through institutional programmes to achieve the final goal of rehabilitation. As a matter of fact, the rehabilitation programme starts from the moment an offender passes the threshold of the prison and undergoes various stages of institutional training. In this process, community services are utilised not only in the management of institutional programmes but also other facets of the entire correctional cycle. The prison manuals of different states and union territories contain provisions for boards of visitors consisting of non-official members which can offer suggestions for the improvement of treatment and training methods in prisons. The manuals also provide for appointment of social and moral education lecturers in prisons. Such lecturers are selected from the community by the state authorities on the basis of their knowledge and ability to influence the prisoners' outlook on life. The All India Jail Manual Committee set up by the Government of India in 1957 had recommended that a review board should be constituted in each state with some non-official members. This board can review cases of inmates of prisons and evaluate inmate's response to imprisonment, training and treatment. After assessing the progress of the inmates in respect of the institutional impacts, the review board recommends to the State Government conditional and unconditional release of a prisoner.

The post-release problems of prisoners are mainly dealt with by voluntary after-care organisations. Discharged prisoners' aid societies in some states have been rendering valuable services for the rehabilitation of ex-prisoners in society. The All India Jail Manual Committee, 1957-59 suggested a network of after-care organisations to be established in collaboration with the people in the community. In fact, the voluntary social workers can assuage the society's feelings of vengeance for the wrong-doers who are in need of acceptance and sympathy after undergoing imprisonment for years together. They are social advocates for ex-convicts and the members of the community. The entire efforts of the community social workers should be directed to reduce the social distance between the ex-convict and the society. The experiment with the open prisons initiated in several states for providing an effective community-based treatment of offenders, has heralded a new era in the field of correctional services in the country.

In the framework of the existing law including the Probation of Offenders Act, 1958, a wide discretion rests with the court in respect of release of offenders on probation under specified circumstances. It has been amply realised that treatment in the open community is preferable to incarceration in prisons where a person is likely to be contaminated by his association with hardened criminals. One acute problem in Indian jails is that different categories of prisoners like under-trial prisoners, short-term and long-term prisoners are kept together. About 63% of the total prisons population consists of under-trials and about 85% are short-termers. One of the most compelling prerequisites of prison reforms is to convert this harmful heterogeneity of the prison population into some reasonable measure of homogeneity. The first important problem is that of reducing the existing short-term prisoners by releasing them on probation of good conduct on a selective basis for treatment in the community. Short-term imprisonment has no therapeutic or rehabilitative value. It only causes over-crowding in jails and gives rise to the problem of social stigma to ex-prisoners. It also leads to economic hardship and distress to the dependents of the prisoner. Therefore, an offender may be selected for release on probation of good conduct and returned to the community on the basis of his personal traits and character. Instead of being a parasite on society, he becomes a useful member and makes his contribution either through his gainful employment in the community or through his participation in the family life.

It is highly desirable that the people of the community realise the usefulness of the community-based treatment of offenders and extend whole–hearted support to this programme. The All India Jail Manual Committee, 1957-59 had aptly recommended that there should be no sentence of imprisonment under three months imposed by the court. This aspect has been realised to a great extent in the United Kingdom where the number of persons sentenced to imprisonment for less than three months in 1970 was just 1200 as against 12000 in 1960. Obviously, a concerted effort was made in that country to use all possible alternatives to imprisonment to achieve this 90% drop. The extensive use of probation and other non-institutional methods by courts in that country played a very important role in reducing the prison population. Similar measures should be taken in our country to reduce the constant increase of short-term prisoners. However, in this matter, an active interaction between the court, the correctional department and the public is essential to achieve the goal.

The inadvisability of short term imprisonment has also been accepted in the Indian Penal Code (Amendment) Bill, 1972. This bill makes provision for certain new punishments, such as externment, payment of compensation to victims, corrective labour and public censure. These alternatives can be purposefully adopted by courts for certain categories of offenders in keeping with their personality traits, socio-economic background and capacity to respond to various modes of correctional treatment. In this connection, probation service needs to be expanded and streamlined to cope with the increasing quantum of probation work. An assessment of the existing probation services in the country reveals that the number of probation officers is extremely meagre. Active public support and cooperation in the field of probation is, therefore, essential for the implementation of the programme.

The Probation of Offenders Rules of various states and union territories provide for the appointment of voluntary probation officers and placement of probationers under the care and supervision of voluntary welfare organisers. Besides supervision of probationers, services of voluntary probation officers may also be utilised in supervising those who are prematurely released from institutions under conditions of good behaviour. The Assam Probation of Offenders Rules provide that for the purpose of the probationer's rehabilitation, the probation officer shall endeavour to secure for him contacts and associations with normal individuals and congenial organisations like Boy Scouts and Girl Guides, youth organisations and community projects. The same Rules further provide that the probation officer shall participate, whenever possible, in after-care schemes and organisations. Similar provisions exist in the Madras, Punjab and Rajasthan Probation of Offenders Rules. These Rules enhance the scope of coopera-tion of people as voluntary probation officers in implementing rehabilitative programmes for offenders in the community. The Bihar Probation of Offenders Rules provide for a probation committee in each district including not less than five non-official members. Similarly, the Kerala Probation of Offenders Rules provide that there shall be a standing advisory committee in each district and one committee including three non-official members at the State-level for enlisting public cooperation and for advising on efficient administration of the Act. The Karnataka Probation of Offenders Rules also makes provision for the constitution of a probation advisory committee in each district including non-official members representing recognised societies, industrial concerns, employers of labour and other social workers in the area to make suggestions for improvement of the arrangements regarding the working of the Act and to secure public cooperation in the handling of probationers and their rehabilitation.

In the implementation of the Borstal Schools Acts which provide for establishment of institutions for detention and training of adolescent offenders, people's participation once again plays an important role. At present, there are eleven borstal schools in various states in the country. All the Borstal Schools Acts make provision for constitution of visiting committees with non-official members appointed by the respective state governments to visit the Borstal Schools either individually or collectively and to make such suggestions for the improvement of training therein as are considered necessary and to report to the State Government, or to the Inspector General of Prisons from time to time any matter, which, in their opinion, should receive attention. The committee is also empowered to consider cases of release on licence and such action as may be necessary in regard to the inmates whose control and detention period is about to expire. Thus, voluntary workers from the community have opportunities to take an active part in the sphere of treatment and training of adolescent offenders.

The Suppression of Immoral Traffic in Women and Girls Act, 1956 has been amended as the Immoral Traffic (Prevention) Act, 1986. It envisages a comprehensive scheme to grapple with the problem of immoral traffic in women and girls by penalising the traffickers, controlling the activities of prostitutes and rehabilitating those rescued from the vice. Voluntary organisations like the Association for Social Health in India are assisted by the Government to undertake preventative programmes against prostitution. The Act provides for public participation in a variety of ways. It provides that the State Government may associate with the special police officer a non-official advisory body consisting of not more than five leading social workers of that area to advise him on questions of general importance regarding the working of the Act. Further, it makes provision that before conducting a search, the special police officer shall call upon two or more respectable inhabitants of the locality to attend and witness the search. Similarly, this Act provides that in discharging his functions, a magistrate may summon a panel of five respectable persons, three of whom shall, whenever practicable, be women, to assist him. The State Government may also issue a licence to a person or an authority for establishing or maintaining an institution as provided under the Act. It empowers the State Government to set up a board of visitors for any local area to visit once a month the institutions situated within such an area and advise on matters affecting the administration of such institutions. This provision gives enough scope for active peoples' participation in the supervision and management of institutions.

Legislation for the prevention of a social evil is not an end in itself. It is only a means and only constant cooperation between the law enforcement agencies and the public at large can make it effective and fruitful. Involvement of the public is, therefore, basic for the successful implementation of the Act. It may be mentioned that the practice of dedicating girls to the temples of Yellamma, Durga and Mungesh in some parts of Karnataka, Maharashtra and Goa is still prevalent and this system has degenerated to such an extent that a large number of dedicated girls who are called Devadasis have finally landed in brothels. The Bombay Devadasis Prevention Act, 1934 and the Madras Devadasis (Prevention of Dedication) Act, 1947 could not help much in the absence of any public support. For any law to be really effective, it should be backed by the willing consent of the majority of citizens. In other words, where a legislation, particularly a social legislation is not supported by a deeply felt and widely expressed public opinion, its effect in terms of compliance is bound to be diluted and sometimes even nullified.

As a part of the preventive programme, voluntary organisations can launch a drive through the length and breadth of the country to counteract harmful publications and pornographic literature, drug abuse and alcohol, sex appeal in movies, etc., which have contributed to various forms of disorganisation resulting in social and moral degradation. In the wake of the growing industrialisation and consequent urbanisation, multifarious problems have cropped up. The joint-family and other social institutions which had so long provided shelter and security to the members in society, are gradually disintegrating. Moreover, the bane of dowry continues to be rampant in society, responsible for shattering the marital bliss of a good number of girls. They neither stay married nor get employed and this sometimes forces them to go astray. In view of such a predicament, mohalla *samitis* consisting of local citizens and representatives of voluntary welfare organisations can play a prominent role in controlling such aberrations.

In the field of beggary prevention, community participation is all the more necessary to create public awareness through the length and breadth of the country about the futility of misplaced charity. Beggary thrives in various vulnerable areas like holy places, places of historical interests, tourist centres, etc. It is possible for a band of dedicated social workers to initiate and continue the tirade against this festering social evil. The existing legislative measures for people's participation touch only the fringe of the curative aspect of the problem. The preventive aspect of the problem should also receive greater attention.

The Narcotic Drugs and Psychotropic Substances Act, 1985 provides for the appointment of an Advisory Committee by the Central Government to be called "The Narcotic Drugs and Psychotropic Substances Consultative Committee" to advise the Government on matters relating to the administration of the Act as and when required. It further provides that the committee may constitute one or more sub-committees and may appoint to any such sub-committee any person including a non-official who is not a member of the committee. Thus, the Narcotic Drugs and Psychotropic Substances Act also provides ample scope for public participation in the over-all administration of the Act.

Now the question arises whether the extent of public cooperation in the implementation of different Acts is adequate. The answer does not seem to be very encouraging. The public at large are ignorant about the utility of correctional programmes and as such there is no effective public cooperation in the implementation of these programmes. Other reasons are the dearth of voluntary organisations and a lack of interest among qualified correctional personnel. However, the importance of imparting short-term training to voluntary workers engaged in the field of crime prevention has been realised by the Government. The National Institute of Social Defence which is a central organisation under the Ministry of Welfare initiated a scheme for training voluntary workers in various aspects of the prevention of crime and the treatment of offenders. In a wide public education campaign, the press, television, radio and audio-visual publicity department have a great role to play. The mass-media may be used to inform the public about the importance of various crime prevention programmes. In other countries like the Netherlands, Sweden and the United Kingdom campaigns are conducted to enlighten public opinion by means of exhibitions, articles in the press, films, television and radio broadcasts with great success.

In the field of correctional services, it is essential to involve the community in a big way for the smooth rehabilitation of the offender back into society. After release from an institution, he finds it difficult to resettle in the community without any assistance. A sort of contempt and inimical feelings often stands in the way of his going back to the community for living as an honest and reformed person. Under such hostile situation, the people of the locality to which he belongs, should come to his rescue and also shoulder the responsibility of dealing with the problems of crime prevention and rehabilitation of offenders. The solution of these stupendous problems lies with the community itself. It may be possible to establish at various levels, people's councils or boards to grapple with these problems right from the apprehension of an offender to the final disposal of his case on the lines of the *Nyaya Panchayat System* of Community justice.

Chapter 2

JUVENILE DEVIANCE

DEVIANCE AND SOCIAL CONTROL

Of late, the word 'deviance' has evoked a lot of interest, particularly in the context of the present changing social milieu. Behaviour is deviant when it violates norms. Thus, deviant behaviour is behaviour that violates the normative rules, understanding or expectations of a social system. Delinquency or crime is the prototype of deviance in this sense. Normative rules are inherent in the nature of all social systems, whether they be friendship groups, families, work teams, factories or societies. But legal norms are those whose violation constitutes deviant behaviour. It ranges from waywardness to serious behaviour disorders, from minor infractions to blatant violations of law. It is a way of responding to the human situations. It involves the whole biological make-up, intelligence, emotional response, cultural environment and interactions with other human beings.

Any statutory violation becomes the subject of official action and is labelled as delinquency. The important factors which are mainly responsible for delinquency are (1) emotional factors, (2) economic factors, (3) environmental factors and (4) personality factors. Delinquency is always an individual problem with the child and anyone coming in contact with him. Generally, unhappy home, uncongenial environment and social disorganisation affect the juvenile's conduct, ideals, attitudes, interests, emotions and physical and mental health. Poverty may not be a direct cause of deviance or delinquency, but its unwholesome impact on the child may be disastrous.

Moreover, the concomitant factors like feeling of inadequacy, frustration, and emotional insecurity play a dominant role in giving rise to anti-social feelings in the child. Every child is born with the desire of being wanted, loved and understood. As it grows, it expects to have an increasing sphere of affection from the mother, father and other members of the family. In fact, there are four basic needs of the child, namely, need for security, response, recognition and development. From the family the child gets physical and emotional support. It provides a safe harbour for him when he moves out alone into the world outside his family. He can return to it whenever frustrations, trials and tribulations outside are more than what he can bear. On the contrary, if his basic needs are not adequately met at home he feels frustrated and seeks to derive satisfaction from any other source. At this juncture, deviance and anti-social tendencies of a child set in. Often he goes out of home and comes in contact with unscrupulous persons and starts pandering to anti-social activities. Potentially anti-social urges exist in every human being. Such urges develop if the child is not brought up in a congenial atmosphere during his infancy. In the early years of the child, the personality patterns are built up for good or bad by his emotional relationship with his parents and others. In fact, the behaviour pattern of his parents has a great influence on him. It is through his early association with his parents that he forms his concepts of right and wrong. This sense of right and wrong is termed as super-ego, i.e., conscience. According to Freud, during the whole of man's later life, the super-ego represents the influence of his childhood care taken and education imparted by his parents.

Now the question arises as to how to deal with the problem of deviance, how to control it, even if it be well-nigh impossible to eradicate it. The enormity of this problem has been causing concern all over the world. Even in the developed countries this problem has assumed alarming proportions. In India, it is gradually becoming acute in the wake of industrialisation and urbanisation in the country. At the same time, cities have grown with their heterogeneous population, high mobility, disrupted relationships, loss of extended family bonds and overcrowded conditions which have a baneful effect on the prevailing value-system and some of the established social institutions. People especially juveniles are largely affected by these changing conditions. They have been socially maladjusted and psychologically disturbed in this labyrinth of changing values. In view of such conditions, the problem of deviance or anti-social tendencies is rearing its ugly head. It may be seen from the statistics available from the 'Crime in India 1991' published by the National Crime Records Bureau, Ministry of Home Affairs, Government of India, that a total of 12,588 crimes were committed under the I.P.C. by the juveniles and youthful offenders during 1991 as against 15,230 in 1990. Similarly, the volume of juvenile crime per one lakh of population was 1.5 for 1991 as against 1.8 for 1990. The following table brings into focus the estimated mid-year population, total cognizable crime under the I.P.C., total juvenile crime under the I.P.C., percentage of juvenile crime to total cognizable crime under the I.P.C. and volume of juvenile crime per lakh of population for five years:

Year	Population in lakh (estimated mid-year)	Total cognizable crime under IPC	Total juvenile crime under IPC	%age of juvenile crime to total cognizable crime	Volume of juvenile crime per lakh of population
1987	7814	14,06,992	52,610	3.7	6.7
1988	7966	14,40,356	24,827	1.7	3.1
1989	8118	15,29,844	18,457	1.2	2.3
1990	8270	16,04,449	15,230	0.9	1.8
1991	8496	16,78,375	12,588	0.8	1.5

In addition to the above position in respect of cases under the I.P.C., a total of 22,143 cases against juveniles under various local and special laws were registered during 1991, indicating an increase of 49.6 per cent over the previous year. Thus, although juvenile crimes under the Indian Penal Code declined by 17.3 per cent in 1991 over the previous year, these had increased by 49.6 per cent under the local and special laws during the same period.

However, it is not possible to assess the exact magnitude of this problem with the available official statistics as juvenile anti-social activities are still dealt with through the traditional social control system. As a matter of fact, the problem of deviance among juveniles is due to a multiplicity of factors which hamper their normal growth in the community. It is necessary to bring them back into society as decent law-abiding persons through a specialised judicial process. This policy has been translated into action mainly through the implementation of the Juvenile Justice Act. Such legal measures are only one kind of social control. According to Marshall Clinard, all groups and societies contrive ways of dealing with unusual behaviour that falls outside their norms. Sometimes, negative sanctions as penalties are imposed on those who violate norms and positive sanctions such as praise or recognition are also bestowed on persons for their commendable works.

Further, some types of social control are formal, i.e., official, while others are informal or unofficial. Formal controls are generally exercised by some official apparatus established under the law. Thus, enforcement and implementation of a law rests with an elaborate machinery like police, judiciary and correctional services. For centuries, men restrained themselves from undesirable actions in the community by various informal procedures. Nowadays, the law has generally flourished in urbanised areas while there are some contemporary societies in rural areas where traditional informal social controls still prevail. For example, in some tribal societies, especially in the north-eastern region, the informal social control system is even now prevalent in a rudimentary form. A very small percentage of delinquent acts in such areas are reported to the police or referred to any other official agency. Most of the reportable anti-social activities hardly come to the surface for official action.

Formal social control through legal measures is comparatively a recent development in human history. In India, Hindu and Mohammedan laws were in force before the British rule. None of these laws had any specific reference to juvenile delinquents. There were, of course, certain ethical codes concerning treatment of children. During the Moghul period, the Koranic precepts were mainly followed in dealing with any kind of anti-social behaviour. In the beginning of the latter half of the nineteenth century, the then Government of India felt the need of enacting laws pertaining to children. In 1850, the Apprentices Act was passed as an all-India measure. It provided for dealing with children between the ages of 10 and 18 years who had committed petty offences or were destitutes. This Act authorised magistrates to commit such children as apprentices to employers who could impart training in some crafts. The objective of the Act was to divert the misdirected energies of juvenile offenders and destitutes who were in crime-prone situations towards learning of some trades so that they might eke out a living on their own after completion of a particular training. Then the Reformatory Schools Act was passed in 1876 which was later modified in 1897. It provided that youthful offenders might, at the discretion of the sentencing court, be ordered to be detained in a reformatory for a period of three to seven years instead of undergoing a sentence of imprisonment. This Act went further to provide that the superintendent of a reformatory might permit any youthful offender who had attained the age of 14 years to live under the charge of any trustworthy and respectable person or any officer of government or a municipality, being an employer of labour and willing to receive and take charge of him on condition that the employer should keep such youthful offenders employed at some trade, occupation or calling. Thus, these Acts initially played an important role in evolving new methods for dealing with deviant juveniles in the community itself under controlled relationships.

Section 562 of the old Code of Criminal Procedure made a specific provision for offenders under 21 years of age for release on probation of good conduct under certain conditions instead of sentencing such persons to imprisonment. Later on, Children Acts were passed by various States in the country with a view to providing for custody, treatment, training and rehabilitation of children who came in conflict with laws. The Government of India also passed a Children Act in 1960 for enforcement in the Union Territories. However, there was no uniformity in the provisions of these Acts. So the Juvenile Justice Act was passed by the Government of India in 1986 which is applicable to all the states and the Union Territories except Jammu and Kashmir. One of the important provisions of this Act is the setting up of two agencies at the trial level to deal with deviant juveniles, and neglected juveniles separately. The juvenile court deals with those who come in conflict with laws while the Juvenile Welfare Board deals with children who are found neglected and uncontrollable. The aim of this provision is to segregate the neglected from the delinquent and to provide treatment and training to the different categories of children separately. This process helps not only in preventing the non-delinquent from coming into contact with the delinquent but also facilitates the proper maintenance of institutional discipline. Moreover, specific needs of different types of children are to be recognised as they are passing through the stages of growth and development. The basic idea behind the juvenile court and the Juvenile Welfare Board is that of guardianship of the state acting for the welfare of children who are of immature understanding at an impressionable age. The juvenile offender is treated not as a criminal but as a ward of the state and receives care and protection. Truly speaking, the fundamental principle of the juvenile court is not to determine whether a child has committed a specific offence but to discover whether he is in need of special care and protection of the state. Thus, the saving of the child is more important than the vindication of the law. In Sweden, the Child Welfare Councils do not find it even necessary to prove the existence of the offence. The role of the magistrate in the juvenile court is, therefore, crucial. He is expected to function as a friend, philosopher, and guide for the child brought before him. There are a number of dispositional alternatives with the juvenile court in deciding cases of children. It may allow the child to go home after admonition or release him under the care of his parents, guardian or a fit person executing a bond for a specific period.

The Juvenile Justice Act, 1986, provides for institutions like special homes and juvenile homes where general education, vocational training and recreational facilities, etc., are available. These institutions not only provide the juvenile with safe accommodation and maintenance but also facilities for his all round development. This Act also provides for the establishment of observation homes as places of safety for children while their cases are pending before the juvenile court. These institutions not only offer facilities for physical security, clean environment and healthy living, but also provide opportunities for closely observing the child and prescribing his treatment and training requirements in accordance with his aptitude and other personality factors. The probation officer plays a significant role in the observation home. Whenever a child is apprehended by the police, the police officer immediately communicates to the probation officer concerned the particulars relating to the child to enable him to initiate social investigation. To make a thorough inquiry into various factors including the social background of the child, the probation officer has to be conversant with the sociological and psychological aspects of the problem of juvenile delinquency and he should have an understanding of human nature. His report on a total situation of the child including his parents, neighbours, teachers and employer, if any, is a corner-stone in the diagnosis and treatment programme of the child. The juvenile court is as such guided by the socio-economic and cultural factors relating to the child rather than by the gravity of his offence.

When a child is released from an institution, he is often confronted with a wide range of adjustment problems. The Juvenile Justice Act, therefore, provides for the establishment of after-care organisations to take all such measures as may be conducive to the rehabilitation of the discharged inmates of institutions. After-care organisations set up by the government or by voluntary agencies may render valuable services in helping them to make smooth adjustments to their post-release environment and lead an honest, industrious and useful life in the community. A well-planned after-care programme also provides for a sort of control over juveniles released from institutions and minimises the possibility of recidivism.

It has been found that the conventional method of institutional services is not adequate in dealing with the problem of crime and delinquency. Even if the Juvenile Justice Act is fully implemented in all the areas of the country, the problems of destitution, vagrancy and begging will persist. In urban areas, particularly big cities, there are some children who do not come under the purview of this Act. For dealing with the cases of such children, it is necessary to introduce non-institutional community-based services which aim at utilising community resources for social control. Hence, greater emphasis is laid on non-institutional method of treatment such as probation, parole, work centres, foster care, adoption and the like. During the Third Five Year Plan, the Government of India formulated a scheme of non-institutional services for the prevention of juvenile delinquency and vagrancy to be implemented in the major cities. The objective of the scheme is to wean away the potential delinquents, vagrants and beggars at an early stage by providing services of recreation, education, counselling, guidance and instruction in crafts with some monetary incentives. It has been amply realised that anti-social tendencies like delinquency and vagrancy are developed by children during the early part of their childhood mainly due to neglect and passive attitude of their parents. Efforts are, therefore, made to deal not only with the child, but also the family, surroundings, school and the community as a whole which affect his upbringing and give rise to anti-social tendencies. This scheme has so far been implemented in six cities. Moreover, juvenile guidance bureaus have also been set up in some cities like Bombay, Hyderabad, Delhi and Madras to provide preventive services to both maladjusted children and their families. Other such schemes include police boys' clubs, bal bhavans, etc., in a few cities.

The rising trend of juvenile anti-social tendencies can be held in check if a comprehensive programme of social action is properly introduced. In view of the large-scale migration of people from rural areas to urban areas, the traditional social control system has given way. It is, therefore, necessary to evolve a new system to enlist cooperation of the people of a particular area. All concerned people like parents, teachers, social workers and law-enforcement authorities of the area may be brought together and a local citizen's committee constituted for each area to effectively deal with the problem of juvenile deviance at the community level itself. Generally, people have a passive attitude towards such problems and are averse to initiate any remedial action. If people actively participate in the programme of citizen's committee, it will generate awareness and a sense of responsibility among the people of an area for tackling the problem of juvenile social maladjustment through their joint efforts.

SERVICE FOR CARE AND PROTECTION OF JUVENILES

The Geneva Declaration of the Rights of the Child of 1924 and the Universal Declaration of Human Rights adopted by the United Nations in 1948 highlighted the importance of the child and maintained that motherhood and childhood were entitled to special care and assistance and that children, whether born in or out of wedlock should enjoy the same special protection. It was further elaborated that the child must be fed, nourished and protected against every form of exploitation and must be given the requisite means for its normal development so as to enable it to devote itself to the service of its fellow beings. The Directive

Principles of State Policy in the Constitution of India also provide under Article 39(1) that the State shall, in particular, direct its policy towards securing that childhood and youth are protected against exploitation and moral and material abandonment.

Similarly, in 1974, the Government of India adopted the National Policy Resolution for Children which spelt out the various measures to be taken and the priorities assigned to the children's programmes. The resolution further explained that children who were socially handicapped, who became delinquent or had been forced to take to begging or were otherwise in distress, should be provided facilities for education, training and rehabilitation so that they could become useful citizens in the years to come.

The problem of orphaned, destitute, neglected and delinquent children is gradually assuming an alarming proportion as the age-old social system has undergone a change and social disorganisation and maladjustment have taken place. The rapid growth of cities with heterogeneous population, occupational differentiation, cultural variations and overcrowded conditions has also accentuated the problem. The Government of India enacted the Juvenile Justice Act in 1986 which repealed the erstwhile children Acts of various states to provide for uniform and comprehensive services for the care, protection, treatment, development and rehabilitation of juveniles in uncongenial situations of social maladjustment, abuse and exploitation. Various child care institutions have been set up to provide amenities and opportunities for physical, mental and emotional growth of such children. At present, there are about 269 observation homes, 249 juvenile homes, 40 special homes and 51 after-care homes under the Juvenile Justice Act, 1986.* In addition to these institutions, there are about 700 destitute homes run by voluntary organisations in the country with financial assistance from the Government. However, the type of institution to which a child is committed depends upon the need of the child. Different categories of children with behavioural problems are sent to closed institutions with proper security arrangements. Such special institutions are generally run by the Government and necessary arrangements are made for imparting vocational training along with literacy education. Destitute and neglected children have no such

*Source: Annual Report 1992–93, Ministry of Welfare, Government of India.

behaviour problems. They can be sent to open institutions providing for literacy education and vocational training either in the institution itself or in outside institutions with proper facilities.

In an institution, the chief needs of the child relate to his physical, mental and emotional development. The basic needs are food, clothing and shelter which are to be met satisfactorily. In a natural home, the child is wanted and receives natural warmth, love, affection and physical care. Even in a poor home the child gets emotional support although all his material requirements may not be available to the fullest extent. Therefore, an institution can never become a substitute for a home with congenial atmosphere. For this reason, a variety of alternative programmes like adoption, foster care, sponsorship and probation are proposed to be developed to enhance the role of the family and the community. However, a large number of orphan, destitute, neglected and delinquent children who have no such facilities, have to be kept in institutions and through the institutional programmes their problems are to be handled. It is in this context that the institutional programme for improving the care, welfare, training and treatment services and maintaining minimum standards assumes paramount importance. A minimum level of services are prescribed and below this level, services are not allowed to fall.

The minimum standard for institutional services can be determined in terms of the physical plant and the services to be rendered to the children admitted therein. The minimum standards in this respect relate to the building accommodation, per capita floor area, playground, assembly hall, library, study room, dispensary and sick room, garden, safety measures, sanitation, lighting, ventilation, drinking water supply, disposal of garbage, drainage system, bath rooms and lavatory, storage facility, fly-proof kitchen, dining hall, recreation room, counselling and guidance room, workshop, classroom, etc. In fact, an institution should be set up at a place away from the congested areas of a metropolitan city. The area should be congenial with natural surroundings. At the same time, the institution should be well connected by various modes of communication. As regards the institutions under the Juvenile Justice Act, the location of such institutions, particularly observation homes, will depend on the case-load of neglected and delinquent juveniles committed by courts in a particular area. It is also necessary to ensure that technical institutes like polytechnics, industrial institutes and educational institutions are located near the child care institutions so that the inmates may easily avail themselves of the benefit of instructions and training imparted in such centres. Moreover, the building of an institution run by the government or voluntary organisations should be in keeping with its diversified programme of training, education and individualised treatment on scientific lines. The plan of the building should take into account a number of factors : (1) the type of children to be accommodated, (2) the programme content of the institution, and (3) the minimum standards to be observed for accommodating the beneficiaries. The minimum space per inmate in a dormitory should be 40 sq. ft. Similarly, other units like classroom, workshop, recreation room, bathroom, sick room, etc., should have sufficient space to cater to the needs of the requisite number of inmates. In accordance with the United Nations Standard Minimum Rules for the Administration of Juvenile Justice, there should be special institutional arrangements for confinement of inmates bearing in mind the differences in types of offenders, offences and institutions.

The Government of India initiated a scheme for providing services to abandoned, neglected, orphaned and homeless children. To promote family atmosphere, the scheme provides for cottage type accommodation with 25 children under the charge of a house mother. In addition to it, the Government of India formulated another scheme for the prevention and control of juvenile social maladjustment and prescribed a minimum standard of services to be maintained in institutions established under the Juvenile Justice Act. Under this scheme, some guidelines in respect of building accommodation with facilities for sanitation and hygiene have been spelt out. A staffing pattern for the effective implementation of the scheme has also been suggested. In view of the nature and magnitude of the work entrusted to the members of the staff in the institution for children under the Juvenile Justice Act, it is essential that such staff should be adequately trained so as to enable them to discharge their functions efficiently. Thus, the United Nations Standard Minimum Rules for the Administration of Juvenile Justice provide that professional education, in-service training, refresher courses and other appropriate modes of instructions shall be utilised to establish and maintain the necessary professional competence of all personnel dealing with juvenile cases. The Government of India framed a set of Model Rules under the Juvenile Justice Act, 1986 which provides inter alia that the State Government shall provide for training for personnel of each category of staff in keeping with their statutory responsibilities and specific job requirements. The training programme shall therefore, include (a) training of newly recruited staff, (b) refresher training courses for every staff member at least once in every five years and (c) the staff conferences, seminars, workshops, etc., at various levels of personnel. The Model Rules further provide that only such persons as are adequately trained in social work should be recruited for the posts of Superintendent, Probation Officer and Case-worker.

In any institutional programme, the period immediately following the admission of a child is of fundamental importance because it is at this stage that he receives his first impression of the institutional life and comes into contact with the staff of the institution. It is during this period that the diagnostic procedures essential to the planning of the treatment and training programme have to be put into operation. At this stage, the educational level and the vocational aptitude of the child are assessed on the basis of tests and interviews conducted by the teacher, the workshop supervisor, the psychologist and other specialists. It is necessary to have a well-equipped classification centre attached to each child care institution run by the Government or by the voluntary organisation. At this initial stage, if the aptitude of the child is not correctly assessed and wrong diagnosis is made, it spells disaster for the child. He may be assigned to a craft which is not in keeping with his innate aptitude and liking. As a result, he fails to excel in the trade and cannot acquire necessary skill for the ultimate rehabilitation in the community. The Model Rules framed under the Juvenile Justice Act, therefore, provide that a classification Committee shall be constituted in each juvenile and special home consisting of the Superintendent, Deputy Superintendent, psychologist, Medical Officer, Workshop supervisor, instructor in vocations, teacher, head of care-taking staff and the officer-in-charge of the reception unit. This Classification Committee is to meet periodically to consider and review (a) custodial care, housing, place of work and type of supervision required, (b) individual problems of juveniles, family welfare, family contacts and adjustment, etc., (c) vocational training and opportunity for employment, (d) education, recreation, group work activities, guidance and counselling, (e) prerelease preparation and planning, post-release rehabilitation programme in collaboration with community-based after-care agencies. These Rules further provide that a juvenile shall be classified on the basis of his age, physical and mental health, length of commitment, degree of delinquency and his character. These apart, factors like possibilities of his being a contamination risk, requirements of custody, his educational and vocational needs, possibilities of his social adjustment, his prospects after release and his rehabilitation needs are taken into consideration. Accordingly, the classification committee plays a very important role in the institutional programme. As a matter of fact, the success of the programme depends on its efficiency and proper functioning.

Children who are committed to the institutional care are mostly those whose formal education has been inadequate to develop fully their talents and potentialities and as such, they are unable to eke out a living on their own without acquiring the requisite skill in some crafts. As he acquires knowledge and skill in a particular trade of his liking, his personality develops and he gains self-confidence which is the sine qua non for successful rehabilitation of an individual in society. Moreover, the child learns to work in cooperation with the teachers, the taught and the authorities of the institution. This process not only helps in the advancement of knowledge but also prepares the child to face problems in life. Vocational training is, therefore, of vital importance in any institutional programme. The Model Rules under the Juvenile Justice Act provide that diversified programmes of vocational training shall be organised in all juvenile and special homes with special reference to employment opportunities available in the community so as to facilitate rehabilitation of juveniles released from institutions. This aspect of the institutional programme was brought into focus by the Seventh United Nations Congress on the Prevention of Crime and the Treatment of Offenders held in Milan in 1985. While discussing the objectives of institutional treatment and training, it observed that the objective of training and treatment of juveniles placed in institutions is to provide care, protection, education and vocational skills with a view to assisting them to assume socially constructive and productive roles in society.

An institution should have a counselling and guidance unit which will be under the charge of a case-worker. The child's dexterity, aptitude and interests are observed through his activities. Programmes of work and recreation should be organised in such a manner that the staff members of the counselling and guidance unit are able to observe the inmates in their various activities and group situations. The Model Rules under the Juvenile Justice Act provide that case-work services shall be provided in all institutions to deal with the individual problems of the inmates. The services of psychologists and psychiatrists are also availed of preferably by establishing linkages with child guidance clinics, counselling and guidance centres and such other agencies in the community. The rules further provide that the educational programme of the institution shall be developed as an integral part of the educational routine emphasising the academic, health, social, moral and ethical aspects. It is also necessary for healthy all round development of the child, that the institutional programme should include regular physical exercise and recreational facilities. In addition to these activities, an institution should have programmes for the socio-cultural uplift of the inmates such as cultural meets, parents-children-staff meetings, community contacts, visits to outside institutions, excursions, etc. These programmes are essential to provide respite to inmates from the drab and monotonous institutional routine. It is also deemed essential to provide leisure time activities like drawing, painting, clay-modelling, cardboard and paper work, kitchen-gardening, etc., so that inmates utilise their leisure in a constructive manner. For this purpose, each institution should have arrangements for such activities under the hobby teachers on a regular basis.

As regards medical facilities, minimum standards should be fixed in terms of full-time and part-time staff, number of beds, indoor and outdoor treatment facilities, stock of medicines, immunisation, preventive and curative services. As provided under section 48 of the Juvenile Justice Act, 1986, immediate action is to be taken in respect of the inmate who is suffering from leprosy or is of unsound mind or is addicted to a drug. He may be removed by an order of the authority to an approved place set up for treatment of such cases for such period as may be certified by a medical officer.

For balanced, nutritious, wholesome and varied food, the State Government prescribes the diet scale for inmates of institutions in consultation with nutrition experts and an inmate is provided with other articles like clothing, bedding, etc., in accordance with the scales prescribed. To ensure compliance of rules and procedures in all these matters, the State Government provides for necessary staff for inspection. The Women's and Children's Institutions (Licensing) Act 1956 also provides that the State Government may make rules in respect of the management of institutions, reception, care, protection and welfare of women and children in institutions including all matters relating to their diet, clothing, accommodation, training, etc., the inspection of institutions and the discharge of women and children and their transfer from one institution to another. The other Act, i.e., The Orphanages and other Charitable Homes (Supervision and Control) Act, 1960 is a comprehensive Act in respect of control of orphanages, homes for neglected women and children and other such institutions. The unique feature of this Act is that it makes a provision for the establishment of a Board of Control for the supervision and control of homes by the State Government.

As the child will ultimately go back to the family after his release from the institution, he is allowed to go home and stay with his family during school vacation or during festivals or special occasions like marriages in the family, etc. Such leave of absence enables him to keep in touch with his entire family members and the community as a whole. Thus, the Juvenile Justice Act provides that the State Government may release a juvenile from the juvenile home or special home on licence for such periods and on such conditions as may be specified in the licence. He may be permitted to live with or under the supervision of any responsible person willing to receive and take charge of him with a view to educating him and training him for some useful trade. Truly speaking, institutional training, treatment and post-release assistance are a continuous process. The rehabilitation process in respect of the child starts as soon as he is admitted into the institution and continues till he is rehabilitated back into society. There are three phases of such services: (a) planning of institutional care, treatment and pre-release preparation, (b) the period immediately after release from the institution and (c) post-release period. While planning post-release assistance, factors like child's personality, his weakness and strengths, his limitations and capabilities and his rehabilitation needs are taken into consideration. In this respect, the classification committee and the probation officer have a very important role to play.

On the whole, the success of the institutional programme depends on the effective after-care and follow-up services in respect of the inmates released from the institution. The Juvenile Justice Act, therefore, provides for the establishment or recognition of after-care organisations to extend help, guidance, counselling, support and protection to all released juveniles whenever necessary. Similarly, the Women's and Children's Institutions (Licensing) Act and the Orphanages and Other Charitable Homes (Supervision and Control) Act also empower the State Government to frame rules in respect of matters relating to the discharge of children from various institutions.

YOUTH UNREST AND GENERATION GAP

Of late, youth unrest has assumed a serious proportion all over the world. The reason is not very far to seek. The present century has ushered in a new era of scientific developments, rapid changes and mounting problems. Consequently, the age-old social system has also undergone a change. Now the world has considerably shrunk in size and the frontiers of knowledge are expanding without any barrier. This trend has produced a tremendous impact on the pace and tempo of life through the length and breadth of the globe. Moreover, the growth of cities with heterogeneity of population, quick mobility, cultural variations and over-crowded conditions has given rise to new ways of living. The attitude of people in general has also completely changed. The lust for power and pelf has tremendously increased. People have become utterly selfish with myopic vision only. As a result, nobody thinks in terms of others. At present, the common tendency of a person is to seek his own interest at the expense of others' welfare and prospects. The traditional adage "Greater happiness of the greater number" remains in books only. The evils of corruption, nepotism, favouritism and smuggling are rampant which are eating into the vitals of the nation. This is a very uncongenial situation where it is well-nigh impossible for anyone, particularly the youth to remain aloof from the evil influences of malpractices and sinister designs. The youth are affected in an unusual way by these changing conditions. The problems of social disorganisation and maladjustment among the youth have, therefore, become acute. There is a wide-spread demand for bringing about a salutary change in various aspects of life. This is, in fact, a global upsurge and often attended to by violence.

Violence erupts in other spheres as well. It is not a peculiar problem with the youth and students only. Other disgruntled groups of people also rise in revolt for amelioration of their conditions. Thus, the poor and exploited people wage relentless struggle against the affluent. Women carry on agitations for their rights to become equal to men. Nations fight for their independence from foreign domination. In all such spheres, violence breaks out as the extreme means. There is a common craving everywhere for a new order with wholesome conditions to achieve the highest fulfilment in life. The youth revolt is not a new phenomenon. It took place in the past as well. In Germany, young people were active in social and political life since the end of Napoleonic wars. The Red Guards of China and the anti-communist student movement in Indonesia may be cited as glaring examples. In the Southern States of America there was an uprising among the student youth against colour prejudices. Similarly, in Latin American countries, there were disturbances by students over the deplorable academic conditions in universities. As a matter of fact, it was the violent student protest that led to the downfall of the Govts. of Marco Perez Jimenez in Venezuela in 1958; Nobosuka Kishi in Japan in 1960; Syngman Rhee in South Korea in 1960; Menderes in Turkey in 1960; Ngo Dinh in South Vietnam in 1968; Victor Paz Estenssoro in Bolivia in 1963; Ibrahim in Sudan in 1964 and Sukarno in Indonesia in 1967. In the recent past, India also experienced a violent student upsurge over the Mandal Commission report which led to self-immolation, death by firing and wanton destruction of public properties. That turmoil was largely responsible for the unpopularity of the government of Shri V.P. Singh at the Centre and its ultimate downfall.

The youth will be at the helm of affairs and guide the destinies of their respective countries in the years to come. Therefore, they have to make themselves eligible for the great task lying ahead. Gurudev Rabindra Nath Tagore aptly said: "A lamp cannot light another lamp unless it contains oil to burn its own flame." They may have lofty idealistic urges in their minds which are often thwarted by the stark and unpleasant realities of the existing social milieu. They have laudable objectives for social transformation, acceleration of economic development and strengthening the democratic institutions. However, in actual practice, they find to their dismay, that the conditions of the masses remain the same. The people are, by and large, in abysmal poverty, illiteracy and unemployment. Although the National census of 1991 reveals some appreciable progress in the field of literacy, we still have to traverse a long distance. The youth reconcile themselves reluctantly with these circumstances. But their perennial craving for change—the transformation of the existing system of confusion and chaos remains endemic in their minds. They have no guidance—no right direction from the adult to realise their dreams of establishing an eldorado. So frustration and dissatisfaction among them have set in and they divert their youthful energies into destructive channels. This problem has all the more accentuated due to the adult apathy, reticence, drift and indecision. In fact, there are some basic needs of the youth, namely, emotional support, security, recognition of aspirations and development. Failure to meet these needs initially results in dissatisfaction and hostility in the young mind. Potentially antisocial urges exist in every human being and what determines, whether they develop or not, is what sort of guidance and assistance they received from the adults. The youth often fall a prey to the unscrupulous adult persons for their nefarious ends.

In India, the youth are generally not prone to anti-social activities. They are, by and large, amenable to discipline and reason. The potential in each youth is full of promise and remains as an important human resource which needs to be properly mobilised. In the words of Swami Vivekananda: "Strong, vigorous, believing young men, sincere to the backbone, are wanted. A hundred such and the world becomes revolutionised." If this important human resource is not utilised wisely, it will spell disaster for the nation as a whole. As a matter of fact, youth is a very critical period of man's life as the idea of right and wrong is firmly ingrained in the mind during this period. If the young people are neglected during this critical period, they develop a sense of desperateness and do not care to abide by the social norms and values. The leaders and those at the helms of affairs of the country should think in terms of the welfare of the youth, their thoughts, feelings, frustrations, apprehensions and aspirations. Their demand is to do away with hypocrisy in public life and to fashion a future of their choice. Hence, a high priority should be accorded to youth participation in the developmental process.

The problem of youth unrest arises due to a conflict between the old and the young generations. This conflict existed even in the olden days. Every generation strives to achieve a specific purpose of its own and with the achievement of that purpose, it outlives its utility. "The old order changeth yielding place to a new (Tennyson)." The new generation comes into being and starts its activities to fulfil its specific objective in keeping with the changing social milieu. The main reason for the youth revolt against the old is that they are incapable of dealing with the mounting problems of the changing world. According to the younger generation, the old people are devoid of skill, efficiency, understanding and above all, sincerity. They indulge in double standards and duplicity in public life which become a source of utter disappointment for them.

A simple example may make the point crystal clear. The people in authority profess to create a new world order based on humanism and cooperation free from violence and at the same time there are films depicting violent scenes shown over T.V. and other mass-media. Such double standards often lead to confusion and bewilderment among the youth. A yawning gap exists between precept and practice that gives rise to a cynical disregard for the hollow words of the superiors. These apart, the rapid technological advances, swift communication system all over the world, man's conquest of space and the impregnable areas of the earth have expanded the vision of men. This changing scenario has brought about a revolution in the social, cultural and intellectual life. The old people generally want to cling to the age-old values and to maintain a status quo. The young people abhor such ideas and feel a sort of contempt for the old.

They may have some respect for the old people who strive to understand their problems and take advantage of the new developments. Thus, Prof. Sisir Kumar Ghosh of Visva Bharati University opines, "The young are really victims of the breakdown of the system. They did not break it. Actually, they have had no models to look up to, neither in family, nor in school, nor in society. The rottenness of our political bosses is there for all to see. The older generation had a choice and duty to mould and condition them. In this, they have failed. All parents are failures. To be respected you must be respectful." If the young are in fault and go astray, it is necessary for the old to delve deep into the causes and take concrete steps to grapple with the problem. In that respect, the older generation has failed to understand their problems that impel them to take to violence.

There is a climate of indiscipline, defiance of authority and proneness to anti-social activities in the country. This unfavourable trend is prevailing at all levels and in all spheres. A steady erosion of moral and ethical values which hitherto sustained the community life, has also added to the overall deteriorating situation. The young join in senseless and self-destructive activities and in a delirious fury, destroy public properties, burn public transport vehicles and railway carriages, destroy university offices, hold up school and university classes and examinations, etc. In such thoughtless frenzy, they create chaos and impose additional financial burden on the depleted meagre resources of the nation. This tendency towards violence is due to the lack of channels through which the disgruntled youth can ventilate their dissent. One of the remedies to prevent such violent outburst of student youths may be the creation of students' council to open up channels of communication between the students, teachers and the authorities and to provide the students with a sense of participation in the affairs of their institutions. Truly speaking, no effective solution to the problem of youth upsurge is possible unless all the concerned agencies—students, parents, teachers, State Governments and political parties meet at a common forum and provide support to the community by playing their respective complementary roles in the system.

In India, about 75 per cent of the population is below 35 years and approximately 55 per cent below 25 years. Moreover, this country has the third largest number of college students in the world after the USA and the erstwhile USSR. Energies and leisure time of this vast youthful population should be meaningfully canalised into constructive channels. During the national freedom struggle, students and young persons were involved in political movements and played an important role. However, with the attainment of independence, there is no longer any justification for their active role in politics. Thus, in the words of Gandhiji, "Politics has two aspects, theoretical side and practical activities. It is essential for the students to be introduced to the former but it is harmful for them to concern themselves with the latter.... Students should be kept away from party politics." For students, the first thing should come first. They should pursue their studies with sincerity, vigour and implicit devotion under enlightened academic leadership. With this end in view, efficiency of teachers and standards of education should also improve. Better teacher-student relationship needs to be built and proper guidance and counselling provided to students. In fact, respect for the teacher should grow in the minds of students with emotional ties between them. This, of course, depends on the quality of teaching and care and sympathy with which students are treated by their teachers. It is no use blaming the student community only. They are subjected to abrupt changes in the curricula, teaching, examination system, methods of assessment and in short, the whole educational system. Under such circumstances, they suffer most in the period of transition. This situation has also added to the prevailing confusion and feeling of insecurity leading to unrest and discontent. In addition, the influence of alien culture on Indian youth and lack of amenities for cultural activities have indeed accentuated the problem.

Formidable difficulties now faced by students in getting admission into educational and professional institutions in keeping with their individual aptitude and aspiration, bleak prospects of employment and the continuously soaring cost of education have made the situation all the more deplorable. In the developed countries like the USA, problems are different. In the midst of affluence and opportunities, there is an increasing tendency among students to discontinue studies and to take to a wayward life. Teachers and those at the helms of academic affairs should think in terms of the difficulties confronted by the student community in the country and make an endeavour to bring about a change in the prevailing murky atmosphere of uncertainty, disrespect and indifference among students. Through regular counselling and guidance an overwhelming section of the student population can be weaned by the authorities. Instead of indulging in anti-social activities and frittering away their indomitable youthful energies, they may imbibe a positive philosophy, a purpose and a programme of bringing about reforms in the existing situation. There is a dire need for the promotion of democracy, human rights and rule of law. In society there are more quarrels and fights, agitations and unrest, corruption, nepotism and sycophancy than peace and harmony, control and happiness, honesty and uprightness.

The entire social atmosphere appears to be polluted. It has become virtually a sick society. Its track record in human rights and democratic functioning is not at all satisfactory. These deteriorating conditions present the young generation with new tasks and challenges. They will have to gird up their loins to eradicate the lurking evils in society and to usher in a new era of peace and prosperity. For that lofty purpose, there should be enough character to go round. The loss of character is the bane of our society. Without the strong base of moral character, problems will only increase at all levels of our existenc—personal, social, national and international. In the words of Mahatma Gandhi: "Your education is absolutely worthless if it is not based on the solid foundation of truth and purity." In fact, the health of the community can be regained only when the people–particularly the younger generation learn the lesson on character-building and develop an attitude of reverence for life. This can be achieved if there is an end to the exploitation of students by political parties and they are kept free from politics. In fine, the whole problem of youth unrest boils down to two important measures, i.e., the realistic understanding of the problems by the older generation and development of a positive attitude by the younger generation since youth is the period of preparation for the future and not for embroiling themselves prematurely in the fight for ameliorating the conditions.

CHILD BEGGARY

Beggary is an age-old social problem. In ancient societies there was no such problem. In fact, giving alms to persons who had renounced the world, was considered as a noble act of religion. The Hindu scriptures mention begging as a respectable profession of ascetics and vedic students. The Hindu Law givers also attached a great sanctity to the act of begging and prescribed regular begging by Brahmacharis. The house-holders were required to give alms to Brahmins and Sanyasins. Even now, during the sacred thread ceremony, the newly initiated Brahmin boy has to beg alms of his mother.

In Buddhism and Jainism there are references to beggary. The institution of Bhikus in Buddhism and Arhats in Jainism include a group of men and women who renounce the world in the name of religion and live on others' charity and alms. Similarly, in accordance with the institution of Khairat among the Muslims, the Muslim kings and rulers distributed alms and other material requirements to fakirs and sanyasins.

These religious sanctions helped in perpetuating the practices of indiscriminate charity. Begging in the name of religion was, therefore, recognised as a socially approved profession. Although there is a gradual decline in the religious faith, the people are, by and large, very much obsessed with the tradition and continue to support the religious mendicants and helpless persons. Thus, beggary still continues as an institution. It became a social problem with the advance of industrialisation and urbanisation. Traditional forms of social institutions started disintegrating due to economic disruption and natural calamities like floods, famines, epidemics, etc. Scientific developments have produced many fundamental changes and provided new ways of living. In other words, the new system has brought in its wake an unwholesome trend of mobility and fluidity, cultural variations, overcrowded conditions and occupational differentiations. The concomitant result of this trend is a spurt in the number of beggars. In the absence of any means of livelihood, people take to begging. Some beggars take to it due to sheer helplessness while others resort to it as a profession.

Beggars may be broadly divided into two categories: Child beggars and adult beggars. The problem of child beggars has, of late, assumed an alarming proportion. They generally come from rural areas, throng in cities, places of pilgrimage and tourist centres. The lure of easy life and prospects of employment drive them out of their rural habitats and throw them into a plight of uncertainty and helplessness. Thus, the problem of begging by children is of urban nature and has its roots in the socio-economic conditions prevailing in the country.

It is difficult to assess the extent of beggary in the country. No comprehensive survey has been conducted so far. However, a few sporadic surveys were conducted in Bombay, Delhi, Lucknow and Madras which do not reveal the exact magnitude of the problem in the country. The census report also does not reflect the actual size of the beggar population. There is also a sizable population of child beggars in the country which is indeed a matter for great concern. There are other categories of persons like pavement dwellers who are not taken into account as beggars. Thus, the problem of begging by children has assumed an alarming proportion. The Government of India had set up a committee in 1968 to study the problem of kidnapping of children for purposes of begging. A few case studies in that connection revealed that there were organised gangs who enticed children to the nefarious act of begging and exploited them for purposes of soliciting alms from door to door. The committee suggested that stringent measures might be taken to deal with this problem by amending section 363A(1) of the Indian Penal Code so that a minimum sentence of three years could be provided to make the law more effective and deterrent. It was also further emphasised that the definition of begging under section 363(4)(a) should be amended to make it more comprehensive in conformity with the anti-beggary legislation of the States.

The Juvenile Justice Act, 1986 provides for dealing with child beggars who are included in the definition of "neglected child." The Bombay Prevention of Begging Act 1959 as extended to Delhi, provides that if the person dependent on a beggar is a child, he should be dealt with under the Children Act (now Juvenile Justice Act). It further provides that if the dependent person is the beggar's own child who is under the age of 5 years and the beggar is an able-bodied mother not being a contagious leper or lunatic, the child may be ordered to be detained in a certified institution without being separated from the mother until he attains the age of 5 years. The Juvenile Justice Act, 1986 makes separate provision for dealing with neglected as well as delinquent children. The Bombay Prevention of Begging Act provides for penalty or sentence of imprisonment for a term of one to three years for employing or causing persons to beg or using them for purposes of begging. The Juvenile Justice Act, provides that whoever, having the actual charge of or control over a child, assaults, abandons, exposes or willfully neglects the child or causes or procures him to be assaulted, abandoned, exposed or neglected in a manner likely to cause such child unnecessary mental and physical suffering, shall be punishable with imprisonment for a term which may extend to six months, or with fine, or with both. As regards employment of children for begging, the Juvenile Justice Act further provides that whoever employs or uses any child for the purposes of begging or causes any child to beg, shall be punishable with imprisonment for a term which may extend to one year, or with fine or with both. In accordance with the provisions of the Indian Penal Code, the penalty for those who kidnap or maim a minor for purposes of begging is upto 10 years of imprisonment. It is necessary to have an effective enforcement of the existing law against those who indulge in organised racketeering.

There are several causes of begging. The causal factors can be broadly divided into economic, religious, psychological and socio-cultural. These factors may be spelt out as under:

1.	Economic factors	poverty, unemployment, destitution, natural calamities like floods, earthquakes, cyclones, etc.;
2.	Religious factors	religious sanction to beggary on special occasions, philanthropic attitude of the people, the general attitude on life which inclines one to believe in destiny;
3.	Psychological factors	unwillingness to work, preference for a life of drift, craving for easy means of livelihood, frustration, and mental handicap;
4.	Socio-cultural factors	traditional and hereditary occupation, family disorganisation, breakdown of joint family system, orphanhood, desertion by supporters and company of beggars.

Another important cause of begging is the rapid increase of population and consequent pressure on land. A bulk of rural population have been displaced from agricultural land in the absence of any suitable viable subsidiary industry. These people are uprooted from their rural base and driven to begging. The subdivision of holdings coupled with the problems of large families and traditional methods of cultivation is also responsible for the deplorable plight of the rural masses. The joint family system which was a source of security and shelter to its members has given way. Now-a-days, in the event of sudden death of an earning member of a family, all dependent members become helpless and destitute and sometimes take to begging. Similarly, when a person suffers from a chronic and pernicious disease, people feel a sort of contempt for him. It becomes difficult for him to stay in the locality. He finds himself in utter helplessness and leaves for an unknown destination with all members of the family.

In some cases parents allow their children to beg with a view to augmenting their income. Lack of facilities for learning useful crafts and trades in rural areas is often responsible for a large scale unemployment and frustration among people which ultimately in many cases lead to begging. There is no organisation at the rural level to look after the welfare of the destitute, helpless, unattached, abandoned and disabled persons. The people in the community are generally averse to the idea of pooling together the available resources for the welfare of these categories of people. Such passive attitude of the people in the community also gives rise to the problem of begging.

The earliest law in India was the European Vagrancy Act of 1874 which was applicable to the whole of the then British India. But it was actually meant for persons of European origin who were found asking for alms or wandering about without any employment or visible means of subsistence. In fact, there was no all India law against begging as such. Certain sections of the Criminal Procedure Code could be used to prohibit begging. Section 109 of the old Cr. P.C. prohibited vagrancy. A vagrant was defined therein as one who had no ostensible means of subsistence or who could not give a satisfactory account of himself. Similarly, section 133 of the old Cr. P.C. provided for penalty for public nuisance. These were, however, indirect laws for dealing with the problem of begging. There is one direct all India measure to prevent begging but it is limited to railways only. The Government of India passed a rule under the Indian Railways Act, 1941 prohibiting begging in the railway premises and in trains.

There are certain sections in the Bombay Police Act, the Calcutta Police Act, 1866, the Calcutta Suburban Police Act and the Howrah Nuisance Act of 1866 and the Madras City Police Act of 1833 which provided for a fine or one month rigorous imprisonment or detention in a beggar home for persons found begging. Attempts were also made for controlling begging through Municipal Acts. These Acts contain provisions which made importunate begging and exposure of diseased limbs for the purpose of begging, offences. The main purpose of these laws was to prevent annoyance and public nuisance from urban areas.

The subject of beggary as such does not figure under any of the lists contained in the Seventh Schedule of the Constitution of India. It may be relatable either to item 15 of the List III, concurrent list covering "Vagrancy" nomadic and migratory tribes or to item 9 of the List II, State List containing "relief of the disabled or unemployable." However, the programme of beggary control continues to be implemented by the State Governments and the Union Territory Administrations under their respective anti-beggary laws. At present, 16 states, viz., Andhra Pradesh, Assam, Bihar, Goa, Gujarat, Haryana, Himachal Pradesh, Jammu & Kashmir, Karnataka, Kerala, Madhya Pradesh, Maharashtra, Punjab, Tamil Nadu, Uttar Pradesh and West Bengal and two Union Territories of Delhi and Daman and Diu have enforced their anti-beggary Acts. All these Acts provide for the prevention of begging through detention, training and employment of beggars and also for their custody, trial and punishment. Begging is a cognizable offence under the anti-beggary Acts and special police squads operate in areas where the Act is in force. The police can round up beggars and produce them before the court. In passing an order under the provisions of the Act, the court considers the report of the probation officer with regard to age, character, health and circumstances under which the accused was living and if he is found to be a beggar, he is sent to an institution for care, treatment, and training for a period of not less than one year, but not more than three years. Now there are 84 institutions for detention and training of beggars in the country with a total inmate capacity of 13,781.*

*Source: National Institute of Social Defence, Ministry of Welfare, Government of India.

During the Second and Third Five Year Plans efforts were made to provide outlays in the State Plans to enable the states to set up adequate institutional machinery for making the laws effective. Some beggar homes came into existence during the second plan in some states. These have further been developed in the third and fourth plans. Inspite of these efforts, it appears that the existing anti-beggary laws are not adequate to deal with this stupendous problem. The services in this field lack uniformity and standardisation because of the variations in the legal provisions and administrative machineries. Moreover, the approach adopted in tackling the problem is based primarily on punitive devices with very little scope for a diversified treatment and training of various categories of beggars. Analysing the prevailing situation, the Study Group on Begging and Vagrancy appointed by the Planning Commission in 1965 had emphasised the importance of the double-track system and recommended the following measure:

"A policy of penal and quasi-penal approach involving apprehension by the police, production before a magistrate and detention with custodial responsibility is inadequate and wasteful when applied to all beggars and vagrants indiscriminately. The policy of differentiation in approach recommended in the third plan deserves to be developed further. Obviously, a double track system is needed. Some found in the circumstances of begging, need primarily social assistance which has to be made available to them as directly as possible, while others need a correctional approach. In developing a double-track system our country would be in line with the modern trend in the matter."

Inspite of the legal measures by various states, the problem of beggary appears to persist unabated. Begging by people of different age-groups at public places like shopping centres, recreational areas, railway and bus stations, tourists' spots, temples, etc., is very common. It has, therefore, been realised that the existing approach towards beggary control mainly based on punitive measures has failed to yield the desired results.

An analysis of the beggary prevention laws of various states reveals that the institutional programmes under the Acts do not provide for a proper classification, placement and treatment. Various types of persons apprehended as beggars are institutionalised within the same setting, irrespective of their individual needs and rehabilitative requirements. Work programmes do not offer sufficient potentials for economic rehabilitation, particularly in relation to the agricultural background of most of the beggars. After-care is the weakest link in the rehabilitation cycle. Though the Acts contemplate a close coordination with voluntary welfare organisations at various stages of institutional care and rehabilitation process, little has been done to develop this aspect. The situation has led to the concentration in governmental institutions of such persons as could otherwise be handled through community's self-help. This is specially so with regard to children in distress. There is hardly any linkage between beggary prevention programmes and social welfare services available in the open community. In view of such circumstances, the Ministry of Welfare, Government of India has recently introduced a scheme under the Eighth Five Year Plan with the aim of developing a differential approach towards the care, treatment and rehabilitation of beggers by providing facilities for their education and vocational training and engaging them on productive work for their reintegration into society. Voluntary Welfare Organisations will also be involved in the implementation of this programme of beggary prevention.

Child beggary is a symptom of the wider socio-economic problems of under-development and paucity of opportunities of gainful employment for a vast number of people in the country. Therefore, progressive economic development resulting in better employment and improved social services in terms of housing, health, education, etc., will be effective long range remedies for preventing the problem of child destitution and child beggary in India.

Children who are without natural parents or proper guardians or who are without shelter and support, are more liable to be subjected to cruelty, victimisation and exploitation. Therefore, all services for the care of destitute, neglected and homeless children will have a profound impact on minimising child beggary. While orphanages and charitable homes provide shelter for orphans and neglected children, it is necessary to extend the scope of such services with the improvement of standards of care and protection. The services should be organised on scientific lines taking into account the physical, emotional and social needs of deprived children. In the absence of readily available alternatives to institutionalisation, orphans and homeless children are taken care of primarily through institutions. However, it is also necessary to explore alternatives to institutional care such as adoption and foster care programmes. A special legislation pertaining to adoption may facilitate efforts in this direction. All States and Union Territories must enforce the Women's and Children's Institutions Licensing Act, 1956 or the Orphanages and other Charitable Homes Supervision and Control Act, 1960 to ensure that institutions for children are managed along proper lines and that children are not exploited for the purpose of begging.

All services for the care and protection of children who are neglected or found begging should be brought under the provisions of the Juvenile Justice Act. All States and Union Territories should enforce the same with full coverage so that all children who are neglected, destitute, homeless or found begging can be given protection and care under the programme. For the effective implementation of the Juvenile Justice Act in the states, adequate machinery such as juvenile courts, juvenile welfare boards, observation homes in every district and sufficient number of institutions for long-term care of destitute and neglected children found begging, are necessary. There should also be proper after-care and follow-up services for all children who are brought up in institutions to help them rehabilitate themselves in society.

Even if the Juvenile Justice Act is fully implemented throughout the country, it can hardly touch the fringe of the stupendous problem of vagrancy and waywardness of children. Such children may have parents or guardians, who may not be able to exercise proper control over their wards. In some cases, parents may not have time to control undesirable activities of their children. For dealing with the cases of this nature, it is necessary to develop community-based non-institutional services with provision for cultural, recreational and vocational training facilities which may be attractive to them. Such programmes of non-institutional services aims at detecting children who show signs of deviance at the early stage and diagnosing actual problems and offering services for recreation, education, counselling and vocational training. Under this programme, children are not required to be admitted as inmates of any residential institution. They remain with their parents at home and attend the work centre in accordance with their respective assignments. Efforts are made not only to deal with the child but also the family, his surroundings, school and the whole community which affects his upbringing and normal development. Parental responsibilities are enforced through counselling and guidance so that parents or guardians may be aware of the problem and extend their cooperation in dealing with their children.

During the third five year plan, the importance of the preventive services was highlighted. The Government of India formulated a scheme of non-institutional services for the prevention of juvenile vagrancy to be implemented in the major cities. This scheme envisaged that cities with a population of 10 lakhs, below 10 lakhs and 5 lakhs could be covered in phases. Six cities, viz., Ahmedabad, Bangalore, Bombay, Hyderabad, Kanpur and Madras implemented this scheme. The organisation of this scheme includes counselling and guidance, recreational facilities, training cum production centres, community services through contact clubs, etc. The mode of operation under the programme consists of appointing social workers who go out in slums to contact children who are found wayward and neglected and to attract them through counselling to boys' clubs where they can have recreational and other facilities in company of children of the same age-group. These clubs are run by voluntary social workers of a particular locality. Such schemes of non-institutional services should be extensively implemented all over the country so that the problem of juvenile vagrancy may be nipped in the bud.

Coordinated efforts are, however, necessary to streamline the institutional and non-institutional programmes so far developed in private and public sectors. All the concerned departments, viz., Welfare, Health, Railways, Transport, Tourism and voluntary organisations engaged in child welfare should make concerted efforts to deal with the problem of child beggary. Committees at various levels with representatives from the concerned departments and voluntary welfare organisations may occasionally meet and deliberate on this problem in respect of a particular area and suggest measures for further intensification of efforts.

Chapter 3

ADULT CORRECTIONS

INSTITUTIONAL TREATMENT OF ADULT OFFENDERS

Prison is the oldest penal institution for detention of criminals. The age-old idea was to remove an undesirable person from society for a particular period and to keep him in isolation in prison so that he might realise his guilt, repent and learn his ways. This idea was based on the feeling that man committed a crime according to his free will and he had, therefore, to undergo physical and mental tortures in a gaol. Thus, prison had originally custodial functions. There was no programme of treatment and training for prisoners. In course of time, with the advance of knowledge in criminology and other behavioural sciences, the idea gained ground that man committed crime not by his free will. There are various factors which are responsible for his anti-social behaviour. If attempts are made to eliminate unfavourable criminogenic factors and proper training is imparted in any useful vocation to enable him to stand on his own feet, his personality will undergo a change and he will be in a position to go back to society as a decent citizen. This conviction has, of late, led to the reorganisation of prison programmes on systematic lines. Now, prisons are regarded not only as custodial institutions but also as treatment and training centres for those who fall foul with laws.

The objectives of imprisonment have, however, varied from time to time and place to place from mere retribution to deterrence and reformation. The emphasis has now shifted from custody to training and re-education of offenders and from mere isolation to association of prisoners with community. It has been amply realized that the protection of society can only be achieved if the offenders are corrected and reformed while in prison through individualised treatment. In consonance with these objectives, an efficient prison administration, diversified resources and facilities for treatment and training programmes and properly trained personnel are regarded as essential. Against this backdrop, the condition in respect of the implementation of the prison programme is to be assessed in this country.

The prison administration in India is governed by the Central Acts, viz., the Prisons Act, 1894, the Prisoners Act, 1900, the Indian Lunacy Act, 1912, the Prisoners Identification Act, 1920, the Transfer of Prisoners Act, 1950 and the Prisoners Attendance in Court Act, 1955. Under the Constitution of India, prison is a state subject. Each State and Union Territory has its own prison manual based on the Central Acts. In fact, the effort to improve the prison system in the country was made as far back as on 2nd January, 1936 when the first Committee was set up by the British Government with Lord Macaulay as a member on it. Since then, in a number of forums the problems of prison administration were deliberated at length. But no tangible result could be achieved in improving the existing conditions of prisons as a whole. In 1864, the Government of India appointed a second committee to consider the problems of jail management. Then in 1877, a conference of experts was held in Calcutta. Again in 1888-89, the Government of India appointed a committee to examine jail administration. It was the Indian Jails Committee, 1919-20 which first brought into focus the importance of separating the juvenile offenders from the adult offenders in prisons.

This Committee was, indeed, a landmark in the field of prisons and other correctional services in the country. At the outset of the report, it observed that "The Indian Prisons have made notable advances in material aspects of administration, health, food, labour and the like. But they have not made equivalent progress in other directions. Possibly the influence of the Report of 1838 has to this day not been quite exhausted. Whether this be so or not, it is certain the Indian Prison administration has somewhat lagged behind on the reformative side of the prison work. It has failed so far to regard the prisoner as an individual and has conceived of him rather as a unit in the jail administration machinery. It has a little lost sight of the effect which humanising and civilising influences might have on the mind of the individual prisoner and has focussed its attention on his material well-being, his diet, health and labour. Little attention has been paid to the possibility of moral or·intellectual improvement. In consequence, while the results of the Indian prison treatment are admitted generally to be deterrent, they are not generally reformatory. The Committee made some very far reaching recommendations covering all important aspects of prison administration. But unfortunately most of these recommendations could not see the light of the day. After independence, some significant developments took place in the field of prison administration. Dr. W.C. Reckless, a U.N. expert was invited by the Government of India under the U.N: Technical Assistance Programme. He visited India in 1952, and studied the prison system in the country and submitted a detailed report to the Government of India with his valuable suggestions for its improvement.

In 1957, the All India Jail Manual Committee was set up. Meanwhile, another important development had taken place at the international level. The Standard Minimum Rules for the Treatment of Prisoners was passed by the U.N. in 1955 which contained elaborate guidelines for treatment of prisoners. The All India Jail Manual Committee, therefore, got the benefit of the guidelines contained in these rules while preparing the Model Prison Manual. It submitted its report in 1959 with a number of recommendations. The Model Prison Manual prepared by it provided broad guidelines for the State Governments to revise their respective jail manuals. In pursuance of one of the recommendations, the Central Bureau of Correctional Services (now National Institute of Social Defence) was established in 1961 under the Ministry of Home Affairs as a Central Organisation to bring about uniformity in the implementation of policies and programmes in the field of prisons and other correctional services in the country. in respect of maintenance of prisons and treatment of prisoners. Later on, the Central Bureau of Correctional Services was transferred from the Ministry of Home Affairs to the Department of Social Security, now the Ministry of Welfare. It was subsequently reorganised with enlarged functions and renamed as the National Institute of Social Defence.

In 1972, the Government of India appointed a Working Group on Prisons to examine measures for streamlining and improving the jail administration and living conditions of prison inmates. The Working Group studied various aspects of prison administration, viz., overcrowding in prisons, prison buildings, vocational training for prisoners, staff structure and training of prison personnel and made a suggestion for transfer of the subject from State List to Concurrent List. Further, it was recommended by the Group to constitute a National Policy on Prisons so as to have a comprehensive development programme. Again, in 1980, the Government of India set up the All India Committee on Jail Reforms to study and analyse various prison problems.

According to the report of this Committee, there were 76 Central Prisons, 250 District Prisons, 822 Sub-jails, 27 Open Jails and 20 Special Jails. The total capacities of all these institutions were 79,544, 63,654, 26,057, 6,640 and 4,626 respectively. There were also 6 institutions for women offenders, 8 juvenile jails and 11 borstal schools with an inmate capacity of 975, 1827 and 2102 respectively. Out of a total of 1,50,692 prisoners, 92,276 were under-trials. In addition to the under-trial prisoners, there were other categories of unconvicted prisoners such as (1) remand prisoners; (2) non-criminal lunatics; (3) persons under protective custody; (4) persons confined under the preventive sections of the Code of Criminal Procedure and (5) prisoners detained under executive orders under provisions of special legislation.

The objective of treatment is to correct the effects of causative factors of criminality in the controlled atmosphere of the prison, utilising the helpful factors in his personality, family situation, and attitude. This approach helps the prisoner to reconstruct his life pattern with renewed vigour for adjustment to the socio-economic situations and healthy inter-personal relationships.

Medical facilities are provided in prisons for physical examination, and treatment of inmates for ailments. In addition to these facilities, psychiatrists and psychologists help in testing and diagnosing the level of intelligence, aptitude and personality. Their findings are useful in planning for the rehabilitation of a prisoner on the basis of his potentialities. The knowledge of the three R's inspires a sense of confidence in the mind of a person and helps him face the reality of the world with courage and determination. Prisoners may be benefited by literacy classes in prisons. Accordingly modern methods of teaching adults may be introduced in our prisons, which not only help in the adult literacy campaign but arouse confidence and enthusiasm among prisoners. In this programme, there is also scope for utilising the talents of the educated prisoners for teaching the illiterate and the semi-illiterate inmates. This programme envisages adequate arrangements for text-books, classrooms and trained teachers. Libraries, daily newspapers, magazines, debates, recreation, sports, observance of national festivals, etc., are also indispensable ingredients of the programme.

Vocational training is an important component of correctional treatment. The ultimate aim of all institutional training is the rehabilitation of inmates back into society. Vocational training, therefore, helps a prisoner acquire sufficient knowledge of any systematised trade so that he can stand on his own feet after release. The All India Jail Manual Committee, 1957-59, therefore, emphasised that 'correctional institutions should establish liaison with the Department of Technical Training and Vocational Guidance Institutes and Aftercare Agencies. Such liaison would bring in improved efficiency in institutional training projects and practical utility from the point of view of the rehabilitation of inmates.'

At present, prisons are manned mainly by custodial staff. In the majority of the institutions, professionally qualified correctional treatment personnel are not available. Of course, in some states a beginning has been made by appointing social workers as prison welfare officers. These personnel can immensely help prisoners in realising their own drawbacks and remoulding their life-style through the methods of case-work and group-work. As a method of treatment, ties with the family and the outside world should be strong and in this area of treatment, the welfare officer has a very important role to play. Sometimes it so happens that during the incarceration, a prisoner loses contact with his relatives and friends and even his family members. His emotional links get disrupted and he finds no interest in any aspect of the programme in the prison. Under such conditions, it is the task of the welfare officer to get him in touch with his friends or relatives. Frequent visits of friends and relatives may be arranged by him. He may also discuss various problems that the prisoner apprehends, might stand in his way of smooth rehabilitation and assist him in his overall planning particularly at the pre-release stage.

The legal system in our country provides for two types of imprisonment, viz., rigorous and simple. Every prisoner sentenced to rigorous imprisonment is required to work compulsorily, subject to his physical and mental fitness as determined by the medical officer. On the other hand, prisoners sentenced to simple imprisonment are not required to work at all. Under-trial prisoners whose cases are pending with the court, are also not required to work. In this connection, the All India Committee on Jail Reforms observed in its report that almost all under-trial prisoners have to pass their time in a very depressing state of idleness. It therefore, recommended that there should be a separate institution for under-trial prisoners with adequate segregation and security facilities at each place where a Central or a District prison is at present required to accommodate under-trial prisoners.

Remission is granted to a prisoner as an important incentive to self-improvement. It is a concession granted to prisoners by the State Government/Inspector General of prisons/Superintendents of prisons. At present, the types and quantum of remission differ from state to state. The Model Prison Manual provides for three kinds of remission, viz., ordinary remission, special remission and State Government remission. Prisoners are eligible for earning remission for three days per completed calendar month for good behaviour, discipline, interest, effort and participation in institutional activities. It is intended to be an incentive for good behaviour and work in an institution and is an instrument of shortening sentences. There is also provision for pre-mature release of prisoners.

As regards training of prison personnel, each state has its own arrangement for imparting in-service training to jail warders. For other categories of officers like Superintendents, Deputy Superintendents, Jailors, Deputy Jailors and Assistant Jailors, there are training schools at Lucknow, Pune, Hissar and Vallore. The National Institute of Social Defence and the National Institute of Criminology and Forensic Science also organise short-term training courses and seminars for senior level officers from time to time.

Of late, the Supreme Court of India delivered judgements in a number of cases, viz., Mohammed Giassudin vs. State of Andhra

Pradesh (1977), Lingala Vijay Kumar and others vs. the Public Prosecutor (1978), Madhav Hayawadanrao Haskot vs. State of Maharashtra (1978), Sunil Batra vs. Delhi Administration and others (1978), and Sunil Batra vs. Delhi Administration (1979). In its judgment, the highest court brought into focus the deplorable conditions of prisons in the country and emphasised the urgent need for re-examining the policies governing prisons keeping in view the importance of improving the plight of prisoners. In view of these judgments, the report of the All India Committee on Jails Reforms has acquired a great significance. The Committee made a thorough study of the problems of overcrowding, prolonged detention of under-trial prisoners, lack of proper treatment programme, etc., and put forward a large number of valuable recommendations for the improvement of the existing conditions in prisons in keeping with the modern objectives of reformation and rehabilitation of prisoners into society.

PROBATION: A COMMUNITY-BASED TREATMENT OF OFFENDERS

In the correctional frame of reference, probation is a non-institutional treatment method designed to facilitate the social readjustment of offenders. It developed as an alternative to imprisonment. The ineffectiveness and harmfulness of short-term sentences gave rise to this method of non-institutional treatment. Thus, probation is a method of dealing with offenders. It is a conditional suspension of punishment which has also to be supplemented by additional safeguards. These safeguards are: (1) careful selection of persons for probation who, on the basis of personality traits, social environment, etc., represent relatively 'safe risks' from the point of view of society and (2) provision of actual assistance to the probationer in the form of personal supervision and guidance during the probation period. Accordingly, probation can be defined as a method of dealing with specially selected offenders and consists of the conditional suspension of punishment while the offender is placed under personal supervision and is given individualised treatment. There are other definitions as well. The American Bar Association defined 'probation' as a sentence not involving confinement which imposes conditions and retains authority in the sentencing court to modify the conditions of sentence or to resentence the offender if he violates the conditions. The Report of the Advisory Committee on Penal Institutions, Probation and Parole to the National Commission on Law Observance and Enforcement defined 'probation' as a process of treatment prescribed by the court for persons convicted of offences against the law, during which the individual on probation lives in the community and regulates his own life under conditions imposed by the court and is subjected to supervision by a probation officer. The length of the probation period varies and is determined by the court. It further adds that probation is the application of modern scientific case work to individuals, outside institutions, with the authority of the law behind it. It calls for the careful study of the individual and intensive supervision by competent and trained probation officers. Thus, three steps are important in probation: (1) careful investigation of persons to be placed on probation; (2) intelligent and well-considered action by the judge; and (3) skilled supervision of probationers. The Department of Justice, U.S.A. in its report on the Attorney General's Survey on Release Procedures has brought out the meaning and utility of probation. It goes on to say, 'as applied by modern courts probation seeks to accomplish the rehabilitation of persons convicted of crime by returning them to society during a period of supervision rather than by sending them into the unnatural and all too often, socially unhealthy atmosphere of prisons and reformatories. Probation is as such the postponement of final judgement or sentence in a criminal case giving the offender an opportunity to improve his conduct and to readjust himself to the community, often on conditions imposed by the court and under the guidance and supervision of an officer of the court.'

Probation is a method of suspending a penalty so that other methods of treatment may be used. It is, thus, a substitute for penalty. It is basically a judicial function. Probation officers are officers of the court. It is the court which has the legal authority to grant probation, although it often acts on the recommendation of the probation officer. The objective of probation is to spare the offender the stigma and other consequences of conviction. In fact, expansion of probation services has become possible due to the growing realisation that the prison sentence is not the best mode of treatment to ensure the protection of society. Though in some cases imprisonment may be appropriate to deal with certain classes of offenders, there are several others in whom prison sentence may produce deleterious effects. Instead of becoming a useful citizen, he may become a tough and frustrated individual with a propensity for further crime.

Probation represents a distinct break with the classical theory of criminal law. It attempts to deal with offenders as individuals rather than as classes or concepts, to select certain offenders who can be assisted while at liberty to form correct habits and attitudes without a penalty, and to use a great variety of methods for this purpose (Sutherland). Sheldon Glueck opines that 'the characteristic feature of probation is that it enables the offender to remain in the community but at the same time to be under control and guidance. Its essence is treatment through application of scientific case work principles.'

The Morison Committee in England defined probation as the submission of an offender while at liberty, to a specified period of supervision by a social worker who is an officer of the Court; during this period the offender remains liable, if not of good conduct, to be otherwise dealt with by the court. The probationer must give his consent to the making of the probation order and to any requirements contained in it. During the currency of the order, if he is in a breach of any of the requirements or if he commits a further offence, he is liable to be sentenced for the offence for which he was placed on probation as well as for any other offence he may have committed.

Custodial treatment removes the offender from his family and community and suspends his social and economic obligations to them. He becomes a burden upon society. On the contrary, probation extracts from the offender a contribution within the limits of his capacity to the well-being of others, whether it is through his useful employment in the community or through his participation in the life of the family or other social group. In so doing, it minimises the economic and social disruption caused by the probationer's offence. Moreover, probation reduces crime by rehabilitating offenders. Many offenders are made more antisocial by serving terms in prisons where they associate with criminals of various kinds and learn more about how to commit crime. Probation protects them from such criminal associations and helps them to lead normal lives in the community.

The object of probation is the ultimate re-establishment of the offender in the community. The basic idea is that the offender redeems himself and is purged of the offence. The law helps him to help himself to erase the stigma of conviction and gives him the guidance of the probation officer. He is not removed from his family and community and therefore, he is compelled to discharge his social and economic obligations to them. It seeks both to protect society and to make the offender a more responsible person and avoids the damaging effects of the traumatic experience of being placed in jail. Probation is thus the process of the discovery of the man by himself with the help afforded by the law.

There are mainly two supervisory functions of *a* probation officer: protecting the community and helping individuals under care. The probation officer wants to safeguard society against the potential recidivist. At the same time, he hopes to help the probationer become law-abiding and stable. During the probation period, the probation officer maintains contact with the offender to ensure compliance with the rules and regulations and also provides various types of assistance to him. Such help includes finding adequate accommodation, job placement, counselling, etc.

Probation is not only a more effective method of dealing with sentenced offenders, it is also significantly cheaper. The expenditure for maintenance of a prisoner in the prison is quite high. Although all convicted offenders cannot be released on probation of good conduct, a good number of offenders, particularly short-termers may be granted probation, thereby saving a lot of expenditure from the public exchequer.

Development in India

In India, the idea of releasing an offender after admonition was envisaged by the *Smriti* writers as early as three centuries B.C. About 2000 years ago, Brahaspati in his *Dandabheda Vyavastha* dealt with individualisation. The judge had the discretion to give a greater or lesser punishment than that prescribed for the offence. The social status of the offender, his knowledge and education, his pecuniary and other circumstances and all that went to make up his individuality were duly considered in awarding punishment. Although the idea of releasing an offender after admonition is as old as the *Smriti* writers, 'Probation' was first introduced under section 562 of the Cr. P.C., 1898 as an extra-mural treatment method. This section was based on section I of the Probation of First Offenders Act, 1887 which had been replaced by the Probation of Offenders Act, 1907 in England. Under this section, release on probation was limited to offences under the Indian Penal Code punishable with not more than two years' imprisonment. It provided that certain types of offenders committing offences punishable with a sentence of imprisonment for less than two years, could be released on probation of good conduct. The scope of this section was, however, extended with an amendment in 1923. As a result of this amendment, this section provided that first offenders committing offences punishable with imprisonment for less than two years, could be released on admonition. It also provided that suitable first offenders aged below 21 and women when not punishable with death or transportation for life and adult men above 21 years of age when not punishable with a term of imprisonment exceeding seven years, could be released on probation of good conduct. The Indian Jails Committee, 1919-20 made some valuable recommendations which brought into focus the importance of separating children and youthful offenders from prisons. In pursuance of this recommendation, some provinces like Madras, Bengal and Bombay passed their Children Acts in 1920, 1922 and 1924 respectively. Later on, barring the states of Arunachal Pradesh and Nagaland all the states had passed their Children Acts. These Children Acts which are now replaced by the Juvenile Justice Act, provide for probation services for juvenile offenders. Under section 21(1)(b) and (21)(2) the juvenile court may release a juvenile offender on probation in consideration of his character, antecedents, family conditions and prospects of rehabilitation. A child is committed to an institution only when there is no alternative method available for the protection, treatment, training and rehabilitation. The baneful effects of drab institutional life is sought to be avoided as far as practicable. The Government of India decided to enact an all-India Legislation on Probation in 1931. But it was not possible to do so due to some adverse circumstances. Subsequently, in 1934, all the provincial Governments were directed to enact their own probation legislation. In pursuance of this directive, some provinces like Bombay, Madras, C.P. & Berar and U.P. passed their respective Probation of Offenders Acts. But they were not uniform. After independence, the Government of India invited Dr. W.C. Reckless, a U.N. expert to study the prison administration and other correctional services in the country and to suggest measures for the improvement of the existing conditions of these services. One of his recommendations was that probation should be developed to the point of being more important than the jail.

The Probation of Offenders Act was passed by the Parliament in 1958 which is applicable to all the States and the Union Territories. This Act marked a distinct advance over the States' Acts. It has removed the limitation based on age, sex and repetition of offences contained in section 562 of the Code of Criminal Procedure, 1898 and the various States' Acts. Now, release on probation is available to all offenders except those punishable with life imprisonment or death provided they are considered suitable by the court for such treatment regardless of age, sex and previous conviction. Similarly, section 360 of the Code of Criminal Procedure, 1973 provides for release of offenders on probation of good conduct and section 361 of the same Code further makes a mandatory provision on the lines of the Probation of Offenders Act, 1958 that special reasons are to be recorded in certain cases particularly of youthful offenders if such cases are not considered for release on probation of good conduct.

Under this Act, pre-sentence enquiries are mandatory in cases of those below 21 years. The Act, however, does not make calling for a pre-sentence report mandatory in respect of offenders who are 21 years old or above. There could have been several reasons for not making calling for such reports mandatory in all such cases as are covered by the Probation of Offenders Act, 1958. Necessary services for making the reports were not adequately available in several places at the initial stage and there was an inevitable time lag in creating the same. Even now, after the lapse of more than three decades of its implementation, most of the states are not having sufficient number of Probation Officers to cope with the increasing loads of probation cases. Another reason is that in a large number of cases, courts have adequate information even without pre-sentence reports to know whether the probation method is needed or not in a particular case. The report of the probation officer is, however, absolutely necessary in the interests of the offender as well as society and should be considered by the magistrate before he decides whether to treat the case under the Probation of Offenders Act and the Probation Officer must help the offender after release under this Act to overcome his difficulties and reform his ways. To release an offender without proper supervision is exposing society to the risk of the offender repeating his unlawful act and the whole principle of probation may, in that case, be discredited. The Probation of Offenders Rules of various states provide for the administrative set-up in detail and the procedure to be adopted in appointing and assigning duties to the officers at different levels for the proper implementation of the probation programme in a state. The requisite qualifications and general attributes of a probation officer are specially provided under the Rules. The Rules of practically all the states provide for a functionary who is expected to give technical guidance to probation officers in their day-to-day working and exercise supervision over their work in general. Such a functionary is designated variously in different states as the Chief Probation Officer, Chief Officer, Chief Probation Superintendent, Principal Probation Officer, Regional Probation Officer and District Probation Officer. The Probation of Offenders Rules of various States and Union Territories provide that the District Magistrate should exercise supervision over probation officers in a district. But in actual practice, such supervision is only general in nature. For intimate professional guidance in the day-to-day planning, development and execution of work in an area, there is need for a functionary with professional knowledge and experience at the state level. The position in respect of the hierarchy differs from state to state. By and large, the Director of Probation Services or Chief Probation Officer or Chief Probation Superintendent under the Director of Social Welfare or the Inspector General of Prisons remains in charge of the probation programme in a state.

The Probation of Offenders Rules of all the states provide that State Government may appoint for each probation district such number of persons as it thinks fit to be probation officers for the purpose of the Act. These Rules provide that while appointing probation officers, a person should have the following general attributes:

(i) adequate educational attainment;
(ii) good character and personality suitable for influencing persons placed under his supervision;
(iii) maturity of age and experience. A probation officer should not be less than 30 years of age;
(iv) aptitude, zeal and calling for probation work.

Probation is a specialised type of work in the field of correctional services which every person with adequate educational qualification will not be able to perform. It is, therefore, necessary to select persons with such specific qualities and aptitudes in addition to their requisite academic attainments. Almost all the States' Probation of Offenders Rules provide that a salaried probation officer should be (i) a graduate, (ii) not less than 25 years and not more than 40 years at the time of appointment. In fact, the higher age limit has been prescribed to ensure maturity. Another aspect of the qualification required of a Probation Officer is training in correctional administration. The Assam and the Rajasthan Probation of Offenders Rules provide that every salaried Probation Officer, before being entrusted with supervision of a probationer, shall have received adequate training. The Kerala Probation of Offender Rules provide that the Probation Officer on probation shall within the period of probation undergo training for three months under the Chief Probation Superintendent before taking up his duties.

Besides salaried probation officers, the Rules of various States and Union Territories provide for appointment of part-time and honorary probation officers. The Andhra Pradesh Probation of Offenders Rules provide that a part-time Probation Officer shall be:

(1) of not less than 30 years of age;
(2) a resident of the district;
(3) in a position to devote adequate time for the supervision of probationers;
(4) a person having sufficient practical experience in social welfare work;
(5) fully conversant with the provisions of the Act and the Rules.

Similar provision exists in the Probation of Offenders Rules of Assam, Bihar, Kerala, Maharashtra, Orissa, Punjab and

Rajasthan. But the training aspect in case of voluntary probation officers has been lost sight of. In Japan where 50,000 voluntary Probation Officers are working in the field of probation services, there is a systematic training course for volunteers.

The main purpose of the appointment of Voluntary Probation Officers is to enlist public participation and voluntary efforts in the implementation of the probation programme. The re-integration of the offender into the community is better and more securely accomplished if the active interest and support of the local community can be encouraged through their involvement in the field of probation.

The Probation of Offenders Act, 1958, makes a special provision for recognition of societies for performance of probation work. It provides an opportunity for the performance of probation work through voluntary agencies at the local level under the overall supervision and direction of Government agencies. The role of the Government agencies and that of the voluntary agencies should be complementary and not competitive. Both are equally necessary for the proper development of probation work in each area. In this connection, a mention may be made of the Maharashtra State Probation and After-care Association which has been doing laudable work in the field of probation.

In some states there is only one Chief Probation Officer or Chief Probation Superintendent for the whole state who has the entire responsibility for the proper implementation of the probation programme. For providing detailed guidance and assistance to Probation Officers employed in various districts, such officers make a test check of the work done in actual pre-sentence reporting as well as of supervision. They allocate the staff needed among the courts in an area according to the varying case-loads and promote and assist voluntary agencies whose assistance is needed for the development of probation work in an area, mobilise local support for probation work in particular and correctional work in general.

According to the prescribed rules, the monthly progress reports of Probation Officers are submitted to the Chief Probation Officer or Chief Probation Superintendent. The courts are informed only in case of breach of conditions or where a cancellation or modification of supervision orders is needed or the same is to be terminated. The Chief Probation Officer or Chief

Probation Superintendent meets every Probation Officer periodically and examines the case records as far as practicable. He pays attention to the manner in which every probationer under supervision has been looked after, number of times he has been met, and visited by the Probation Officer at home, in office or in his place of employment, the manner in which his family and other difficulties have been handled, etc.

Functions

Regarding the duties of Probation Officers, knowledge and experience needed for their work is not the same in respect of all types of work to be done by them. It is possible to so distribute the work as to utilise the services of some jobs requiring relatively lesser degree of professional ability. Some states like Andhra Pradesh, Karnataka, Kerala and Tamil Nadu have two cadres of Probation Officers Grade I and Grade II. In Bihar, Manipur and Rajasthan there are Probation Officers and Assistant Probation Officers. The basic establishment for a probation area comprises one senior and one or two junior officers.

As regards supervision of probationers, the Probation of Offenders Rules of all the States and the Union Territories provide that the Probation Officers shall act as a friend and guide of the probationer. For this purpose, he shall require the probationer to report to him at stated intervals, meet frequently and keep in close touch with him. However, the frequency of the meetings, including visits by the Probation Officer, depends upon the conduct and mode of life of the probationer and the progress he makes. The number of meetings shall usually be not less than:

(a) once in a week, during the first month;
(b) once in a fortnight during the remaining period of probation in case of probationers below 16;
(c) once in a month during the remaining period in case of others.

The Probation Officer has to endeavour, by example, advice, persuasion and assistance and where necessary, by warning, to ensure that (a) probationer does not violate the conditions of the supervision order or commit any further offence and (b) his behaviour, habits, attitude to society, character, etc., improve so that he may not revert to crime.

The Probation Officer may move the court to vary the conditions of the bond by way of tightening or relaxing them as may be required by the conduct of the probationer. The Probation Officer has to carry out any direction given by the District Magistrate or other officer not below the rank of Sub-divisional Officer and submit reports to the District Magistrate on the progress of probationers as may be required. The Probation Officer has also to report to the District Magistrate in cases where conditions of the supervision order or bond are not adhered to, such as (i) the probationer changing his residence, (ii) any fresh offence committed by the probationer, (iii) any serious violation of the condition of the supervision order, (iv) any plan of the probationer to abscond, (v) any attempt by any person to abet or aid him in the commission of a crime and (vi) any factor obstructing the rehabilitation of the probationer.

The Probation Officer assists the probationer's rehabilitation in society. He endeavours to secure for the probationer (a) facilities, (b) employment opportunities, (c) necessary financial aid and (d) contact and association with normal individuals and organisations like Boy Scouts, Girls Guides, Youth Organisations and Community Projects.

The Probation of Offenders Rules of various states provide that the Probation Officer shall maintain constant touch with discharged probationers to follow up the progress made by them towards their rehabilitation for such period as may be specified by the Chief Probation Officer or the Regional Probation Officer.

In addition to these, there are certain other fields wherein probation services are utilised. These are:

(1) educating the public and mobilising support for the probation system;
(2) mobilising cooperation in the field of social defence;
(3) managing probation homes;
(4) performing such other duties as may be assigned to him by the State Government.

Most of the jails in the country are over-crowded and at times it becomes well-nigh impossible to accommodate the growing influx of offenders in jails. Under such circumstances, the offenders who are convicted and sentenced to imprisonment for short periods ranging from one month to six months should be given chances to receive treatment outside the jail, because such short periods of a few days or months are not sufficient for imparting training to an inmate. On the contrary, during such short periods the convict gets in touch with hardened criminals in prison and panders to vices when he comes out of the prison. Such imprisonment does more harm than good to the offender and ultimately to the community. At present, there are about 880 Probation Officers in the country. There is no fixed case-load per Probation Officer. In fact, in our conditions, the Probation Officer has a heavier task to perform in securing rehabilitation of each case. While making enquiries or supervising cases, areas to be covered in our rural conditions, are very extensive and communications are not easy. The facilities for communications differ from one part of the country to another. The jurisdiction to be covered by an officer in various parts of the country is not of similar size or population. There are some states where one Probation Officer looks after the probation work of the entire district. It is, therefore, necessary to evolve a formula for work-load per probation officer. The National Correctional Conference on Probation and Allied Measures held in New Delhi in 1971 deliberated on this problem and suggested that each Probation Officer should have 125 units of work per month which might be calculated as follows:

(1)	Each pre-sentence enquiry	5 units
(2)	Each supervision case	2 units
(3)	Each miscellaneous enquiry	2 units
(4)	Court attendance	2 units

However, it is not possible to assess the exact quantum of work of the Probation Officer. The posting of Probation Officers in most of the states has no relevance to the actual case-load. Generally, the basis of appointment of a Probation Officer is geographical and one Probation Officer is appointed in a district irrespective of the number of courts. In some states, Probation Officers are also District Social Welfare Officers with the charge of multifarious other works of social welfare. Under such circumstances, unless Probation Officers are appointed on the basis of work-load, the quality of probation work is bound to suffer. Now, the question arises whether there can be a common criterion for work-load of each Probation Officer. In a vast country l' .e India, a common criterion to assess the quantum of work of a Probation Officer cannot be applicable through the length and breadth of the country because of geographical, climatic and communication variations. A Probation Officer in a city may be able to make pre-sentence enquiries of much more cases in addition to supervision than the Probation Officer posted at a far-flung area in the country where communication facilities are not available. There are even now some areas where a Probation Officer has to spend days together to pay a visit to the home of a probationer. Often he has to go by train, by bus and by boat and sometimes on foot. So a common standard in assessing the quantum of work of a Probation Officer is not feasible.

On the basis of statistics for the year 1991*, the number of persons convicted for cognizable offence under the Indian Penal Code annually is 6,35,927. The Probation of Offenders Act does not apply to cases punishable with death or life imprisonment. But the number of persons convicted of such offences constitutes less than 10% of the total number of persons convicted for cognizable offences. If pre-sentence enquiries were ordered by courts, in 75% cases of those found guilty of cognizable offences with an average of 150 enquires per Probation Officer, about 3180 Probation Officers will be required for dealing with 4,76,946 enquiries per annum in the country. Moreover, if 25% of those found guilty are released on probation supervision, there will be a further demand for an increase in the number of probation officers. Further, with the implementation of the Juvenile Justice Act in various States and Union Territories, more Probation Officers for enquiries and supervision will be necessary.

All the states, except Arunachal Pradesh, Nagaland and Sikkim, have enforced the Probation of Offenders Act after framing necessary rules. While Andhra Pradesh, Gujarat, Karnataka, Kerala, Maharashtra and Tamil Nadu have made good progress, other states are still lagging behind. There are some important causes for the unsatisfactory progress in the implementation of the Probation of Offenders Act. The reason for the lack of progress is the indifferent attitude towards probation. There is a tendency to regard the probation service as an ordinary function which any lay person can do without any special aptitude and training. In

*Source: 'Crime in India' 1991 published by the National Crime Records Bureau. M.H.A., Government of India.

fact, at the initial stage, rapid progress cannot be made in the probation programme due partly to the unfavourable and non-cooperative attitude of some concerned agencies and partly to the ignorance of the people. To overcome all these difficulties, the Probation Officer has to put in relentless efforts to convince the judiciary, the police, the bar and above all the people at large of the utility of probation as a non-institutional community-based treatment method. It is a herculean task on the part of a probation officer to organise probation work in a district with several sub-divisions or talukas. The Probation Officer has to keep in constant touch with the court, the police, the bar and the jail authorities. The quantum of work of a Probation Officer cannot, therefore, be judged from the number of cases investigated or supervised. For the development of the Probation Programme, the authorities in charge of probation services at the state level should take some important steps. Firstly, there should be wide publicity about the utility of probation service so that the district level agencies, especially, the judiciary, the police, the jail and the local authorities like municipality, panchayat, etc., may be fully aware of this beneficial programme. Secondly, there should be a probation committee in each district with the District Magistrate as its Chairman. The Committee should include the Superintendent of Police, the Superintendent of jail, the employment officer, a representative of the bar, a social worker, a representative of the municipality, panchayat, etc. Thirdly, probation services should be treated as a specialised field and professionally qualified persons with necessary aptitude should only be appointed as Probation Officers. Fourthly, in order to achieve and maintain scientific standards in probation work and inspire public confidence in its processes, probation service should have a supervisory hierarchy consisting of Chief Probation Officer and Principal/District/Regional Probation Officers for every state with suitable scales of pay and they should have the necessary technical qualifications and professional interest in the development of probation work.

REHABILITATION OF THE DEVIANT

Of late, the problem of rehabilitating the deviant, i.e., the offender, has assumed considerable importance. The age-old idea of inflicting severe punishment on offenders for their reformation has gradually undergone a change. If we go through the history of crime and punishment, we come across horrifying tales of inhuman treatment meted to offenders. Even for a trivial offence, an offender had to undergo barbarous tortures. He used to be dragged in the street, maimed and often beaten to death. In case of imprisonment also, the plight of convicted offenders was deplorable. They used to be huddled together without any facility for classification, segregation, treatment and training. The prospects of their rehabilitation and reassimilation in society were relegated to the background. They were put to hard unproductive work. Thus, the old prison system was designed to crush the offender both physically and mentally. It was based on the idea that rigorous imprisonment with physical tortures would strike terror in the minds of the offenders and ultimately they would realise their guilts, mend their ways and return to society as decent law-abiding persons and continue to behave well under the constant fear of punishment. But, in course of time, this idea proved wrong. Although fear of punishment often serves as a deterrent, it does not help in ultimate rehabilitation and reassimilation of offenders in society. Hence, the basic approach should be the treatment and training of offenders, their reformation and rehabilitation.

It has also been realised that mere treatment in institutions does not help in the ultimate rehabilitation of offenders. It can not bridge the gulf between the institutional experience and the stigma society attaches to the released inmates. Thus, the total punishment for crime never comes to an end after imprisonment. It continues as a life-long record and it becomes difficult for many released offenders to go back to society as decent law-abiding citizens inspite of their sincere and genuine desire to live honestly. The deplorable condition of the convict at the time of his release from the prison has been vividly described by Frederic Wines in his book 'Punishment and Reformation': "The most terrible moment in the Convict's life is not that in which the prison door closes upon him, shutting him out from the world but that in which it opens to admit of his return to the world, having suffered for months or years from the deprivation of pleasures to which he was accustomed, and having little, if any money in his pocket to meet expenses." In many areas of community life the discharged prisoner finds himself handicapped and stigmatised. He is confronted with multifarious problems–psychological, social, economic, legal and the like.

The ex-prisoner feels that he has been forsaken by society, relatives and even by some members of the family. Doubts nag him as to whether any one in the family will accept him. Caught in such a state of uncertainty, he loses his self-esteem and ultimately becomes demoralised. Sometimes it so happens that he is unable to find a shelter at the end of the prison sentence. At this critical juncture of his life, he pines for love, security and help. But nobody comes forward to render any assistance and guidance. It becomes difficult for him to get a job even if he is a skilled worker. The Employment Exchange also does not come to his rescue. He is debarred from getting any job if his previous conviction is disclosed. Sometimes during his imprisonment, his property is misappropriated and he finds it difficult to get it back after his release. What is worse, an ex-prisoner is always kept under surveillance by the police. In case of any theft or disturbance in the locality, the people suspect him and want the police to arrest him. Even if he is in no way connected with the crime, the police often harass him for any slight disturbance in a locality. He needs legal help to prove his innocence at such moments. Under these circumstances, the need of after-care services arises. It is necessary to prepare the prisoner on the verge of his release so that he may be able to rehabilitate himself back into society. In principle, a prisoner is to be contacted within the prison long before his release and his problems ascertained. As a matter of fact, the institutional training and post-release assistance are a continuous process and the after-care services are an extension of the services already rendered in an institution. Thus, the Model Prison Manual prepared by the All India Jail Manual Committee spells out the objects of the after-care services as under:

(a) to extend help, guidance, counselling, support and protection to all released prisoners whenever necessary;

(b) to help a released person to overcome his mental, social and economic difficulties;

(c) to help in the removal of any social stigma that may have attached to the inmate or his family because of his incarceration;

(d) to impress upon the individual the need to adjust his habits, attitudes, approaches and value schemes on a rational appreciation of social responsibilities and obligations and also of requirements of community living;

(e) to help the individual to make smooth adjustments to his post-release environment;

(f) to encourage the individual in making satisfactory readjustment with his family, neighbourhood, work-group and community;

(g) to assist the individual in functioning as self-dependant and self-reliant socially useful citizen;

(h) to assist in the process of the individuals' physical, mental, vocational, economic, social and attitudinal post-release readjustment and ultimate rehabilitation;

(i) to complete, in all respects the process of inmates' final readjustment, resettlement and rehabilitation in the free community;

(j) to treat after-care problems of the individual in their totality and not in isolation. Not only the individual but his whole social situation is to be tackled at the same time.

In principle, efforts for rehabilitation of an offender should begin from the time he enters the prison. A comprehensive prison programme is, therefore, essential to cater to the needs of different categories of inmates. There is also need for improvement in the existing prison programme which should have a salutary impact on the personality of the inmate. He should feel the urge to go back to the community as a decent law-abiding citizen. With this end in view, inmates of various institutions are imparted training in a number of crafts and trades on modern lines so that they may stand on their own feet and eke out a living after their release. Now-a-days, welfare officers are appointed in prisons to help the inmate maintain his contact with the members of his family and explore the possibility of his employment in the community even before his release.

In India, the present prison system was introduced during the British rule. It was Lord Macaulay who first highlighted the despicable plight of inmates in jails and emphasised the need for improving the existing institutional programmes. Subsequently, various committees were set up by the then Government between 1836 and 1920 to look into the multifarious problems of prison administration and to suggest measures for improvement. The Indian Jail Conference of 1877 first discussed the question of helping ex-convicts but no positive steps were taken thereafter. However, a discharged prisoners' aid society was organised as a non-official agency in U.P. in 1894. Similar societies were organised in Bengal and Bombay in 1907 and 1914 respectively. But these societies could not function for long due to the lack of Govt. support and public sympathy.

During the period from 1872 to 1910, a wave of reformation swept the western countries. In India also, the importance of reformation and social rehabilitation of offenders was emphasised. The Indian Jails Committee, 1919-20 highlighted the need for shifting the emphasis from punishment of offenders to their reformation. It went further to stress the need for prison labour as one of the means of reforming the offender. So it recommended that the prison industries should be reorganised so that prisoners might find interest and earn their livelihood honestly after their release. As a result, some changes had taken place inside jails. The provincial governments also initiated steps to provide assistance to the discharged prisoners. The Madras Prisoners' Aid Society was established in 1922 with 21 district committees. The main activities of this organisation included assistance in employment, provision of board and lodging facilities, financial and legal assistance, etc.

Similarly, in Bombay in place of the Prisoners' Aid Society which was organised in 1914, the Maharashtra State Probation and After-Care Association started working in the field. One released prisoners' aid society 'Navajeevan Mandal' is also functioning at Pune. In Bengal, the After-Care Association for Juveniles and Adolescents was set up in 1928 with five branches. The activities of this organisation were mainly concentrated on the maintenance of supervision over the Juveniles and Adolescents released from borstal schools, reformatory schools, industrial schools and juvenile jails. In Uttar Pradesh, the first Discharged Prisoners' Aid Society was established in Lucknow in 1930. The name of this organisation was subsequently changed as the U.P. Crime

Prevention Society which is engaged in the work for employment and rehabilitation of discharged prisoners. In other states also, sporadic efforts were made to provide after-care facilities to ex-prisoners. But, on the whole, these efforts have fallen far short of the actual requirements.

In 1955, the Central Social Welfare Board set up an Advisory Committee on After-Care to assess the extent to which after-care services met the needs of the discharged prisoners and the released inmates of other institutions and to suggest ways and means for establishment of additional services of statutory and voluntary agencies. After a thorough study of the situation, the Committee observed that there was no coordination between the training imparted in institutions and the opportunity of employment available in the community. In consequence, the inmates who are released from institutions feel frustrated. The Committee, therefore, recommended that after-care services should be organised on a national basis. In pursuance of this recommendation, district shelters were brought into existence where discharged prisoners could stay for a short period and receive help to readjust to society. State homes were also set up for men and women where ex-inmates of institutions could stay for longer periods and receive training in various crafts.

The All India Jail Manual Committee, 1957–59 emphasised the importance of after-care services and recommended that these services should be developed as an essential requisite in the correctional field. The All India Seminar on correctional services held in New Delhi in 1969 also recommended several steps to improve the after-care services. The Juvenile Justice Act, 1986 contains a comprehensive provision regarding the establishment of after-care organisations for taking care of juveniles discharged from juvenile homes or special homes and for the purpose of enabling them to lead an honest, industrious and useful life. The Act further provides that the State Govt. should constitute advisory boards to advise on matters relating to the establishment and maintenance of homes, mobilisation of resources, provision of facilities for education, training and rehabilitation of neglected and delinquent juveniles. Statistics for the year 1985-86 as compiled by the National Institute of Social Defence, Ministry of Welfare, Govt. of India reveal that there were about 40 after-care institutions in the country to cater to the needs of the juveniles discharged from various institutions. But, in view of the increasing trend of juvenile crimes in the country, these institutions can touch only the fringe of the problem.

The discharged prisoners' aid societies or any other organisations rendering assistance to ex-inmates of correctional institutions can extend help mainly in two areas: (1) social rehabilitative services, and (2) vocational rehabilitative services. Under the social rehabilitative services programme, these organisations can establish after-care hostels for accommodation of discharged inmates. Truly speaking, these hostels serve as half-way houses and pave the way for smooth rehabilitation of offenders back into society. In some cases discharged inmates find it difficult to get shelter in the community. What is worse, the fear of public contempt haunts them and they hesitate to go back to society soon after their release from institutions. It becomes difficult for them to get employment. The training imparted in institutions is generally inadequate. This is a serious drawback and stands in the way of their rehabilitation. The community is also indifferent to the plight of the ex-convicts and refuses them any help. They are stigmatised and shunned.

A good number of released inmates of institutions may be in need of after-care services for their rehabilitation. For want of adequate after-care services, many ex-convicts cannot avail themselves of these facilities. Although there are a few shelters and after-care homes in certain states, these cannot meet the increasing demands of accommodation. To make the after-care programme effective, it is necessary to have legislation regulating the procedure of admission and duration of stay in after-care homes of ex-prisoners. As things stand at present, discharged prisoners enter and leave after-care homes at their sweet will. There is no legal provision to compel them to stay there for their benefit. On the other hand, some inmates of after-care homes do not like to leave the same even after getting jobs. This situation creates problems for accommodation of new-comers.

In some countries like Britain, the after-care programme has been a good deal successful because prisoners are released from prisons on parole and licence and kept under supervision till the term of imprisonment expires. During this period, the released prisoner has to abide by the rules and regulations prescribed under the law. A large number of such people receive statutory after-care along with those who voluntarily seek after-care. In fact, the after-care service in Britain is fairly comprehensive and embraces all stages of the rehabilitative process. A conscious effort is also made to do away with the stigma attached to an offender through the enforcement of the Rehabilitation of Offenders Act, 1974. This Act provides that any one who has been convicted of a criminal offence and has received a sentence of not more than two and a half years in prison is eligible for the benefit under it. If he is not convicted again during his rehabilitation period, he becomes a rehabilitated person and his conviction becomes spent. If such a system with necessary legislation is introduced in India, the after-care programme for rehabilitation of ex-convicts is likely to make much headway.

The All India Seminar on Correctional Services, 1969 deliberated on this problem and recommended that statutory after-care might be introduced to facilitate rehabilitation of ex-prisoners in society. It may also be possible to integrate probation and after care services in various States and Union Territories in India. In Britain, the probation and after-care committee in each county is able to enlist cooperation of various agencies and the public in an effective manner. Likewise, a state-level probation and after-care committee comprising officials and non-officials may be set up in each state in India. In some states, district probation committees which are already in existence, may consider bringing after-care service as well within their area of responsibility.

Although prisons have acquired a new dimension as therapeutic and training centres for those who come in conflict with laws, they do not serve the purpose of training and rehabilitation of all categories of offenders. As a matter of fact, custodial treatment removes the offender from his family and community and suspends his social and economic obligations to them. He becomes a burden upon the society. Therefore, various non-institutional treatment methods like probation have, of late, assumed great importance. In Britain, there are at present several alternatives to imprisonment available to the Court. These alternative methods include (1) discharge after warning, (2) conditional discharge, (3) probation, (4) community service orders, (5) attendance centre and (6) suspended sentence. Any one of these methods is applied to an offender to avoid imprisonment. An offender is sentenced to imprisonment as a last resort. The non-institutional services have developed tremendously in Britain as the judiciary itself had taken the initiative in implementing the non-institutional programmes.

In Britain, section 15 of Criminal Justice Act, 1972 empowers courts to order offenders to perform unpaid work as a service to the community. It is based on the principle that people who commit minor offences can be better occupied doing service to their fellow citizens than sitting alongside others in an over-crowded prison. While considering a community service order, the Court requires consent of the offender to attend punctually community work assignments under the supervision of a probation officer for a specified period. Such a scheme may be introduced in our country with some changes, if necessary. This system encourages the offender to participate in some constructive work which not only enables him to repay the loss, but also provides him with an opportunity to unfold his latent talent. Through this method an offender is able to rebuild his shattered self-esteem and image as a responsible member of society.

However, while considering the applicability of community service scheme as a non-institutional treatment method to India, we have to visualise some impediments likely to be confronted. Firstly, people are generally averse to the idea of non-institutional services for offenders. There is a common feeling among the public that the non-institutional method of treatment is a device to show leniency towards those who have offended against society. Even after several years of its implementation, the probation scheme does not seem to be widely known to the public. The traditional outlook towards crime and criminals is still persisting and it will take some more time for the people to shake off this attitude. Secondly, it will take considerable time to disseminate the lofty idea of community service scheme through the length and breadth of the country.

It will be necessary to bring home the importance of this scheme not only to the public but to the concerned agencies like the judiciary, police, bar, municipality, village panchayats, etc. Thirdly, paucity of adequate funds may stand in the way of implementing this scheme. In the development planning, correctional schemes generally receive a low priority. Lastly, a majority of offenders are agriculturists and day-labourers who do not have sufficient leisure time to be earmarked for their voluntary work on a particular project. Inspite of these difficulties, it may be possible to go ahead with the scheme. To start with, a section may be added to the existing Probation of Offenders Act, 1958 providing for community service orders. While releasing an offender on probation supervision, the Court may also pass community service orders in some suitable cases. On the whole, the ultimate objectives of probation and community service orders schemes are the same. It may be possible to go in for a new legislation at a later stage.

Chapter 4

STATUS OF WOMEN

CHANGING STATUS OF WOMEN

"There is no chance for welfare of world unless the condition of women is improved. It is not possible for a bird to fly on only one wing."

—*Swami Vivekananda*

Our ancient scriptures contain examples galore in respect of women's prominent roles in society and their participation in multifarious religious, cultural and social functions. The names of Sita, Savitri, Damayanti, Gargi, Maitreyi, Lilawati, etc., are highlighted in the annals of Indian womanhood. By dint of her merit and proficiency a woman could attain a high position in society. However, women have traditionally a status less than men in society. In Hinduism, she was prevented from studying the Vedas or performing any sacrifices. According to Manu, a woman must never be independent. In childhood, she must be under the control and guidance of her father, in youth under her husband and in old age under her son. One of the Manu's Codes goes further to mention that "by a girl or by a young woman or by a woman advanced in years, nothing must be done even in her own dwelling place, according to her pleasure." An ideal Hindu wife is expected to be faithful and submissive to her husband and other relations like father-in-law and mother-in-law, etc. Her qualities of devotion, respect and self-sacrifice are extolled. In the West, William Blackstone's eighteenth century codification of the English common law provides that a husband had the right to physically chastise an errant wife. Such value systems were also prevalent during the Roman Empire and the middle ages. Thus, various societies all over the world supported subjugation of women in one form or another. In Indian epics, there are many legends depicting the despicable condition of women. Ahalya was turned into stone by the curse of her husband Sage Gautama—although she did not consciously commit any wrong. Similarly, Sage Jamadagni's consort Renuka incurred wrath of her husband for no fault of her own. She was bathing in the river 'Varada' when she was distracted by the good looks of a youth. Jamadagni sensed this through his yogic power and ordered his son Parasuram to behead her.

In Islam, men and women are regarded as equal. But in course of time, women were accorded an inferior position in many respects. As a result, a woman cannot become a priest and lead the prayers. Moreover, the practice of seclusion and veiling imposed a restriction on women depriving them of the right to participate freely in community functions. However, there is a declining trend now in such rigidity. As regards marriage, man has unequal rights over woman. The husband is permitted polygamy and has the unilateral right of divorce. Although the bride's consent is required before the marriage is solemnised, it is a formality only. The husband enjoys a higher position as the head of the family and demands obedience and service from the wife. However, widow remarriage and divorce are permitted for women. Some security is also provided to a married woman through dowry. But very few of them can take advantage of this provision. Thus, the interests of women are ignored keeping in view various advantages for the males only. As a matter of fact, monogamy has been accepted in the laws for Christians, Hindus, Parsees and Jews. In other words, a major chunk of the Indian population, i.e., about 88% is legally governed by the same principle. Only the Muslim law remains still unchanged. It is high time that it should also be reformed so as to fall in line with that of all other communities in India. Of course, there are obstacles in bringing about uniform legal reforms in this respect. The glaring example is the Shah Bano case of 1985 in which the Supreme Court gave momentous verdict in consonance with the latest trend. But some sections of people in that community raised hue and cry as a result of which the decision of the apex court was reversed.

The practice of monogamy among the Christians has raised the status of women in that community. Moreover, among the

Catholics and some other groups divorce is not permitted. So, women in that community have greater sense of security and independent moral entity. They can participate in all religious ceremonies. However, the fact remains that inspite of such latitude, women's inferiority to men persists in that community as well. In the Parsee community, women enjoy a position of honour in the family and society. They have rights to property, religious and cultural activities. They are also permitted to divorce and remarry. However, a Parsee woman marrying outside their religious faith, is not allowed to participate in religious activities or enter the fire temple.

It transpires from the above discussions that there is, by and large, no radical difference in the position of women in any religion. In the 19th and 20th centuries, reform movements were launched by the Brahmo Samaj and the Arya Samaj among the Hindus and similar movements in other communities against the evil practices like child marriage, etc. were also started. However, the leaders of these movements could not make much headway because of vehement opposition from the orthodox sections in all communities. Iswar Chandra Vidyasagar had to encounter fierce opposition from the fundamentalists in Hindu society while he was making relentless efforts to introduce widow remarriage. Raja Rammohun Roy also launched a vigorous tirade against the evil practice of Sati in Bengal and ultimately succeeded in getting it abolished through legislation. Very few social legislations could, however, be enacted during the 19th century as the then British Government were reluctant to interfere in social and religious matters in India.

The evil effects of child marriage were highlighted by the social reformers. Consequently, the Civil Marriage Act fixing the minimum age of marriage at 14 was passed in 1872. Later, the Child Marriage Restraint Act, 1929 fixed the minimum age for marriage for males at 18 and for females at 14 which was subsequently amended as 15. This Act made the practice of child marriage a penal offence for parents or those performing, conducting or directing it and for adult bridegrooms. But the validity of such marriages was left untouched. As a result, the lofty purpose of the Act could not be achieved. The Act should, therefore, be amended so that such marriages may be declared as legally void. The Special Marriage Act, 1954, fixes the minimum age at

21 and 18 for males and females respectively. In accordance with the Muslim Personal Law, a girl has the right to repudiate a child marriage. Similar provision may also be made to introduce the 'option of puberty' in the Child Marriage Restraint Act. The offences under this Act have been made cognizable in the State of Gujarat. Child Marriage Prevention Officers are also appointed there to enforce the provisions of the Act. Despite these persistent efforts, in a tradition-ridden society, it becomes difficult to enforce such a social legislation as the machinery itself cannot get rid of the traditional outlook. In order to put an effective check on child and bigamous marriages, there should be compulsory registration of marriages as recommended by the U.N. Of course, registration of marriages is compulsory for all marriages performed under the Special Marriage Act, 1954.

The Dowry Prohibition Act, 1961 which is an important social legislation, could not achieve its purpose due to a lack of public awareness. This evil can be reduced or ultimately eradicated if social conscience is awakened. There are many cases of ill-treatment of girls by their in-laws for failure to bring adequate dowry. Statistics available from "Crime In India—1990" published by the National Crime Records Bureau, Ministry of Home Affairs, Government of India, reveal that 4602 persons (3769 males and 833 females) were arrested for committing crimes under the Dowry Prohibition Act in 1990 as against 4078 persons arrested during 1989. Thus, there is an increasing trend in the incidence of these crimes. This problem can be solved to a considerable extent through increasing avenues of employment and economic freedom for women. Side by side, the Act should also be enforced vigorously with necessary infrastructure as provided thereunder.

The incidence of divorce is the highest among Muslims followed by Hindus, Buddhists, Jains, Sikhs and Christians. Some of the common grounds for divorce are adultery, barrenness and extreme poverty. The Hindu Marriage Act, 1955 provides for divorce to both the parties for (1) living in adultery; (2) conversion; (3) cruelty; (4) insanity; (5) communicable disease like leprosy; (6) venereal disease; (7) renunciation; (8) disappearance for seven year or more; (9) failure to resume cohabitation for two years after a decree of judicial separation and (10) failure to comply with a decree for restitution of conjugal rights. In addition to the above, a wife has two additional grounds for divorce: (a) If the husband has another living wife; and (b) if he has been guilty of rape, sodomy or bestiality. But the position in the Muslim law is different. A husband has an absolute and unlimited right to repudiate the marriage at his will. On the contrary, a Muslim wife has no such right. Her position remains inferior and insecure. The Indian Divorce Act, 1869 which governs all Christians, also discriminates between the husband's and the wife's right to seek divorce. The husband can divorce the wife if she has committed adultery. In case of the wife, she has to prove a second offence of adultery by her husband in order to obtain a divorce. However, the Special Marriage Act, 1954 provides that divorce can be obtained by either party for adultery, desertion for three years, cruelty, unsound mind, leprosy, venereal disease, continuous absence for seven years, non-resumption of cohabitation for one year following a decree of judicial separation or non-compliance of a decree for restitution of conjugal rights. Besides these grounds, a wife can obtain divorce on the ground of rape, sodomy or bestiality.

As regards adoption and guardianship of children, the legal position of a woman is on the whole inferior. The Hindu Minority and Guardianshp Act, 1956 upholds the superior right of the father and makes him the first natural guardian of boys and unmarried girls. The mother has, however, the prior right to custody of a child below five years of age and in case of an illegitimate child, she has a better claim. In fact, the welfare of the child is of paramount importance in such cases. In pursuance of a Supreme Court decision, the mother could be the natural guardian even when the father was alive depending on the circumstances of the case. On the other hand, a Muslim father's position is dominant and his rights in respect of guardianship of a child are very wide. The mother is not entitled to become a natural guardian even after the father's death. However, she has prime rights to custody of minor children. The Guardian and Wards Act, 1890 is not applicable to Hindus and Muslims. It provides that the father's right to guardianship of a child is primary and no other person can be appointed as a guardian unless the father is found unfit. In view of such discrimination and inequality prevailing in various societies all over the world, the U.N. Commission on the Status of Women recommended the equality of rights and duties between men and women in respect of guardianship of minor children. Likewise, the National Committee on the Status of Women, 1971-74 set up by the Ministry of Social Welfare, Government of India also recommended: (1) that the control over the person and property of a minor cannot be separated and should vest in the same person; (2) that the question of guardianship should be determined entirely from the point of view of the child's interest and not on the basis of prior right of either parent; (3) that the parent who does not have guardianship should have access to the child; and (4) that the child's choice of guardian should be obtained when he reaches the age of 12.

The all-round development of a society requires full participation by all sections of the population including women. The provision of opportunities for full development of the potentialities of women is all the more important. This principle is explicitly enshrined in the U.N. Declaration on the Elimination of Discrimination Against Women. As a matter of fact, the age-old social handicaps from which women suffered for long, are no longer impediments in the way of improving their status in society. Moreover, the mounting problems in the changing society have made it essential for women to participate in multifarious activities and share higher responsibilities. The traditional practice of excluding women from labour outside the family is still prevalent in some sections of society and there is a social stigma on the working women as well. Some people emulate this traditional practice to enhance their social status. It should also be borne in mind that a large number of women are unpaid family workers whose contribution to the family's earnings is not generally recognised.

The latest technological development has brought in its wake demands for new skills and know-how. Women are generally not well-equipped with these skills. They are in need of training to improve their earning capacity, especially in the lower income groups. At present, Government as well as voluntary agencies are engaged in imparting informal training to such women. The Central Social Welfare Board has introduced schemes for assisting training-cum-production centres in small scale industries and handicrafts. Some Ministries like Agriculture and Community Development, Health and Family Welfare, Human Resource Development (Department of Women and Child Development) have also developed welfare centres to improve women's earning capacity through training in sewing, embroidery, tailoring and handicrafts. These training programmes have made only a marginal impact on the employment needs of women as there is no planned link between production and marketing. The creation of a separate Department (Women and Child Development) under the Ministry of Human Resource Development is a welcome step in the right direction. The national objective of integrating women into the development process at all levels in keeping with the guarantees enshrined in the Constitution can be achieved if congenial social condition is created and help extended to women for performing effectively their multiple roles as housewives, mothers and socially and economically productive individuals. In consideration of special problems of women, opportunities should be provided for part-time employment with necessary safeguards against exploitation. Facilities of child-care services should also be made available to all working women. The problems of accommodation and security of such women are often acute. The working women's hostels which are being set up during the Five Year Plans, although inadequate, will go a long way in solving this problem.

For improving women's status, the role of education has been emphasised all over the world. The Indian social reformers of the 19th century also realised the importance of education in this respect and a small number of women started participating in social welfare activities outside their homes. In the early twentieth century, some women's organisations sprang up to carry on the movement for their political rights. In 1917, Shrimati Sarojini Naidu led a deputation of Indian Women to present a demand to the British Parliament for the enfranchisement of women on the basis of equality with men. But the result was not fully satisfactory. The Reforms Act of 1921 extended the franchise only to those women who had property and education. In 1930, a meeting of representatives of the women's organisations demanded adult franchise without sex discrimination. It was subsequently accepted by the Karachi Session of the Indian National Congress in 1931 and that resolution could see the light of the day only after independence when the lofty principles of equality and dignity of the individuals were enshrined in the constitution. Thus, Article 39(d) of the Constitution introduced a new dimension opening new vistas for women to play their roles in the political, economic and social spheres. This newly emerging trend could not, however, change the attitude of the people substantially. The traditional myopic view still persisted. Hence, the subsequent measures in respect of academic planning and allocation of resources for the uplift of women were tardy and to some extent perfunctory. Inspite of a phenomenal expansion of the formal educational system, a large majority of Indian women have remained illiterate. Of course, the female literacy rate has increased from 0.69% in 1901 to 24.82% in 1981. Simultaneously, their literacy rate in rural areas has gone up from 13.08% in 1971 to 17.96% in 1981 and in urban areas from 42.05% in 1971 to 47.82% in 1981. Now Kerala has the highest female literacy rate being 65.73% in 1981.*

It is essensial to mobilise public opinion and strengthen social efforts against gender injustice and campaign for women's awareness. The mass media has an important role in changing the attitude of the people in the needed direction. It is common knowledge that films, advertisements and pornographic literature depict women as sex symbols often contributing to sex crimes and deviant behaviour. Such unscrupulous activities degrade the image of women and impair their status in society. This unwholesome trend should be reversed and the media apparatus used meaningfully to generate public awareness of the urgent need for women's equality, dignity and status in society.

The condition of female prisoners has not so far received much attention. Their statistically meagre number has been a hindrance to the development of any progressive action to ensure custodial and processual justice to them. In fact, there has been continued neglect and discrimination against them at all stages of the criminal-correctional process. At present, there are about 1280 prisons in the country. Of these, only six prisons are exclusively for women with a total capacity of 975. Moreover, the annual average female prisoner population is about 4000. It can, therefore, be inferred that only about a fourth of the female prisoners can take advantage of the existing institutional facilities. As far back as in 1919, the Indian Jails Committee for the first time brought into focus the importance of setting up separate institutions for women prisoners. Since then, the need for separate institutions for them has been emphasised at various forums. The All India Committee on Jail Reforms, 1980-83 expressed concern

---

*Source: 'Women in India—A Statistical Profile—1988' published by the Government of India, Ministry of Human Resource Development.

and observed that "while living conditions, treatment and training for male prisoners are nowhere near the desired level, the lot of women prisoners is much worse." It further opined that "in view of the status of women in the family and society, their special needs and problems and their vulnerability while in prisons, special consideration has to be given to the segregation, protection, care, treatment, training and rehabilitation of women offenders." The Committee had recommended, *inter alia*, that a women's non-official organisation might be set up to look into various issues: (1) revision of legislation in respect of women prisoners; (2) establishment of homes for released women prisoners; (3) action against atrocities committed against women in prisons; (4) reintegration of ex-women prisoners into the family and community; (5) provision of free legal aid to women prisoners; and (6) welfare of prisoners' family.

In view of the present unsatisfactory plight of female prisoners, the National Expert Committee on Women Prisoners, 1986-87 recommended that it was necessary to formulate a National Policy on custodial justice to women in keeping with their rights, dignity and status in custody. It went further to suggest that a statutory autonomous body should be set up with representatives from each component of the criminal justice system and other allied disciplines like medicine, psychiatry, law, social work, etc., to review the implementation of the proposed policy. Since the beginning of this century, efforts have been made to improve the conditions of prisons in the country by setting up committees and working groups and a plethora of recommendations also find place on record. Truly speaking, the main problem is the problem of implementation. If women in crime are to be saved and gender justice achieved, appropriate measures are to be taken in conformity with the latest trends in corrections which aim to eradicate the cause of crime rather than the criminals by educative, corrective and reformative methods.

In fine, it may be reiterated that equality of women is necessary as a basic condition of social, economic and political development of the nation. Disabilities and inequalities of which women are victims, cannot be removed by women only. This movement should form part of a total movement for removal of all inequalities and indignities prevalent in society and special tribunals to deal with all violations of human rights, discrimination against women, protection of women's rights in society, should be set up as recommended by the National Committee on the Status of Women, 1971-74.

FEMALE OFFENDERS AND THE PROBLEM OF GENDER JUSTICE

The number of female offenders is generally meagre and the problem of security is also not acute in their case. As a result, no meaningful efforts were so far made to improve their conditions in custody or after their release from institutions. They have been subjected to continued neglect and discrimination at all stages of the criminal-correctional process. Thus, the National Expert Committee on Women Prisoners, 1986-87 had aptly observed that "an intrinsic factor contributing to neglect of women in custody or offender women is the apathy generic to various disciplines to take up women separately as subject of specialised enquiry." In fact, the prison laws which are almost hundred years old, are not in keeping with the present trends in corrections, let alone the improvement of the conditions of female prisoners. At present, there are 1280 prisons in the country. Of these, only six are exclusively for women with a total capacity of 975 and the annual average female prisoners population is about 4000.* Only about a fourth of the women prisoners as such can take advantage of these institutional facilities. It was in 1919 when the Indian Jails Committee for the first time brought into focus the importance of setting up separate institutions for women prisoners. Since then, the need for separate institutions for female prisoners has been emphasised at various forums.

Most of the undertrial female prisoners are lodged in seperate enclosures of common jails. The All-India Committee on Jail Reforms, 1980-83 expressed concern and observed: "It hardly needs to be argued that the principles underlying their confinement, should apply to their female counterparts also with necessary adjustment of details issuing from sex differences. The fact, however, is that while living conditions, treatment and training for male prisioners are nowhere near the desired level, the lot of

---

*Source: Report of National Expert Committee on Women Prisoners, 1986-87.

women prisoners is much worse. Women in prisons as we have witnessed during our visits to various jails in different states and union territories suffer from unhealthy living conditions, exploitation, unnecessary prolonged severance from their families and lack of gainful and purposeful employment." The Committee further opined that "in view of the status of women in the family and society, their special needs and problems and their vulnerability while in prisons, special consideration has to be given to the segregation, protection, care, treatment, training and rehabilitation of women offenders." It made a number of important recommendations on various aspects of treatment and training of female prisoners.

This Committee also suggested that a women's non-official organisation at the national level be set up to look into the following issues:

i) Revision of legislation in respect of women prisoners;
ii) establishment of homes for released women prisoners;
iii) action against atrocities committed against women in prison;
iv) re-intergration of ex-women prisoners into the family and community;
v) supply of free legal aid to women prisoners; and
vi) welfare of prisoners' family.

The prevailing system of accommodating different categories of prisoners in the same prison has led to a lot of problems, especially in respect of women prisoners. While dealing with the problem of classification and segregation of female prisoners, the Indian Jails Committee, 1919-20 opined that "it is not only desirable to separate the convict from the unconvicted prisoner but it is also most necessary to keep female adolescents away from older prisoners, habitual from non-habituals, and prostitutes and procuresses from women who have lived hitherto a respectable life." Similarly, the All India Committee on Jail Reforms, 1980-83 highlighted in its report that "segregation of offenders on the basis of sex, age, criminal record, social background, and sequence of criminal behaviour is an essential feature of modern prison system. But during our visits to various states and Union territories we observed that undertrial prisoners, prisoners sentenced to short, medium and long terms of imprisonment, prisoners sentenced to simple imprisonment, habitual offenders, lifers, hardened and dangerous prisoners, children, young offenders, women offenders, civil prisoners, prisoners sentenced by court martial, criminal and non-criminal lunatics, detenus under the National Security Act, persons detained under the Conservation of Foreign Exchange and Prevention of Smuggling Activities Act, smugglers, etc., were all kept in the same institution and the arrangements for their sergregation even in different wards were not effective." The National Expert Committee on Women Prisoners, 1986-87 had also brought into focus this problem and stated that "in defiance of the basic correctional tenets, classification of prisoners continues to be non-existent in most prisons except in a few where long-term sentence holders are kept. However, even in the latter, 'mental cases' along with those held under 'protective custody,' are indiscriminately mixed with other categories."

The problem of overcrowding in prisons is due to the presence of a large number of under-trial prisoners. According to the statistics for the year 1987* there were 4791 female prisoners out of whom 1836 were under-trials. Under such conditions, custody of inmates becomes the main concern of the staff and the other aspects like care and welfare of inmates are neglected. The total population of female prisoners far exceeds the existing accommodation available in separate prisons. If any meaningful programme is intended to be implemented the buildings of the institutions should be properly designed and necessary accommodation provided.

It is essential to organise diversified educational programme to suit the needs of different inmate groups. Prisoners should be reeducated and well equipped to assume higher responsibilities in the outside world. Most of the states have introduced educational facilities in central and district jails. In some states, institutions provided facilities to selected inmates for attending schools or colleges outside. Inspite of all these facilities, the education system in prisons needs further improvement in terms of diversification of the entire educational programme so as to cater to the varied educational needs of different groups of prisoners, particularly female prisoners. While discussing the problem of educational facilities for female prisoners, the Indian Jails Committee,

---

*Source: Ministry of Home Affairs, Government of India.

1919-20 observed that "in the exceptional case of a female prisoner who is able to read, arrangements should be made to enable her to get books from the jail library should she desire to do so. It will hardly, we fear, be possible to arrange for regular instruction in the case of female convicts, except where special female prisons are provided."

The National Expert Committee on Women Prisoners, 1986-87 also opined that "both education and work are of proven value to prisoners and have an intrinsic role to play in the reclamation process not only during incarceration but also in the prisoner's rehabilitation after release." The Committee further pointed out that "it is lack of education and work opportunity that are often responsible for the woman's initial arrest as well as her deviance and custodialization." It further observed, "unfortunately, the inducements to advance educationally and to acquire an income generating potential have not found any systematic expression in the Indian Custodial ethos." It may be possible to introduce condensed courses for those who desire to appear in secondary examinations. A majority of the female prisoners may not have the aptitude to go in for higher studies. So there should be an arrangement for training in crafts which are viable in the open community. Side by side, it is also essential to provide cultural and recreational activities in prisons for the benefit of the mental and physical health of female prisoners. The activities break the tedium of drab institutional regimentation and bring in an atmosphere of relaxation and joy. These activities are also intended to inculcate a discipline of healthy interests so that after release the inmate may spend her leisure time constructively. The All India Committee on Jail Reforms, 1980-83 recommended that "suitable recreational programmes should be organised for women prisoners which may include simple outdoor games, bhajans, music, folk dances and dramas. Those who have talent in any of these fields should be encouraged to develop and continue it." These activities have sublime effects on the minds of prisoners and help in congenial personality development.

There should be proper scientific classification of inmates in prisons. It is necessary to draw up a suitable vocational training programme of each prisoner in accordance with her aptitude and interest. The National Expert Committee on Women Prisoners suggested that "in existing prisons where women are in sufficient numbers, a proper classification system must operate which should include medical, criminological and social assessment of the inmate and serve as a basis for specialised and segregated care, treatment, employment, training, education and rehabilitation of the inmates. In existing prisons with fewer inmates, scientific correctional care must be there even if physical segregation is not possible. The classification system should be introduced compulsorily in all prisons and custodial institutions. It should be used as a continuous programming and monitoring device rather than as a one-time activity. Training in some crafts as imparted at present in a number of institutions, has no relevance to the outside demands and as such the woman prisoner has slim chances of getting a job, leading to frustrations. All India Jail Manual Commitee, 1957-59, therefore, emphasised that "correctional institutions should establish liaison with the Department of Technical Training and Vocational Guidance Institutes and After-care Agencies."

As regards medical facilities, female prisoners face problems because male doctors are generally posted in almost all prisons. The National Expert Comittee on Women Prisoners highlighted this fact and suggested that "medical, diagnostic and care facility must be available to inmates routinely; and by a female doctor, where full or part-time women medical staff are ill-afforded, local female doctors from government health facilities must be inducted to serve the prisoners as visiting consultants." The Committee went further to suggest that "schools of medicine should also be required to place women medical interns in prisons for specified periods." Similarly, the All India Committee of Jail Reforms recomended that "there should be a separate ward for women in prison hospitals. If there is no such hospital ward they should be treated in their own barracks by a lady doctor and attended to by the female staff."

A female prisoner has special problems when she is found pregnant. Gynaecological examination needs to be conducted and prenatal and postnatal care taken according to the requirements of each case. A woman prisoner is allowed to keep her child with her in prison till it attains the age of 4 years. However, the age-limit differs from state to state. In some states it is 5 years. The child is ultimately separated from the mother and sent to the members of the family at home or to a relative, if any. During the Third Five Year Plan, a new scheme of welfare services in prisons was initiated as a plan scheme. This scheme included appointment of welfare officers in prisons and setting up of creches for children of female prisoners. The All India Committee on Jail Reforms pointed out the inadequacies in this respect and suggested that children upto the age of five years accompanying women prisoners might be allowed to be kept with them and creches set up for those children outside the main prison building.

During her incarceration, a woman prisoner generally loses contact with her relatives, friends and even her family members. Her emotional link gets disrupted and she finds no interest in any aspect of programme in the prison. Under such circumstances, it is the task of the welfare officer to get her in touch with her friends and relatives. He may arrange for visits of her relatives and family members at regular intervals. He may discuss various problems that the female prisoner apprehends, might stand in the way of her smooth rehabilitation and assist her in overall planning, especially at the pre-release stage.

Although legal aid facilities are now made available in some places, no significant steps have been taken to provide such facilities to women prisoners. In fact, a female prisoner suffers from a lack of knowledge of her basic rights and due to the absence of a legal support system. What is worse, she is generally handicapped because of her illiteracy, low status and inability to mobilise resources. It may so happen that the family may shun her and may not like to come to her rescue. In view of such circumstances, there should be a legal aid unit attached to each prison to cater to the legal needs of women prisoners. The role of the prison welfare officer is also important in keeping them abreast of the availability of the legal facilities. The National Expert Committee on Women Prisoners deliberated on this point and suggested that "to supplement the legal aid personnel, and to inject greater sensitivity to women's custodial situation, women social workers and activists need to be deployed and given appropriate para-legal training which should not only enable them to understand the legal aid processes but also to utilise them to remedy existing lapses. Such a cadre of women workers can be reliably trained to deliver first aid in law to women in need both within and outside custody."

At the pre-release stage, the prison welfare officer's assessment is essential for the prisoner's early release and also in arriving at a decision about her parole. However, the assessment is often delayed due to lack of adequate personnel and procedural reasons. As things stand at present, all the female prisons and female wards of prisons in various States and Union Territories do not have prison welfare officers. In that case, probation officers of the district in which the prison is situated, may make necessary assessment of the prisoners well in time and suggest early release of the inmate or otherwise. The All India Committee on Jail Reforms 1980-83 recommended that special consideration should be given to women prisoners in the matter of their premature release. In the pre-release and post-release programmes non-official organisations, especially women's organisations devoted to the field of welfare of women prisoners should be involved. As a matter of fact, a central committee for the assistance of released women prisoners should be set up in each State and local branches formed for each central and district jail.

After-care service is of paramount importance in the process of training and rehabilitation of offenders. 'In fact, treatment in the prison and after-care should be part of the same process. This process must start as soon as the offender crosses the threshold of the prison and it should continue till the ex-prisoner is fully rehabilitated back into society. The difficulties of an ex-prisoner at this stage are formidable and these are all the more acute in the case of a woman prisoner. The All India Committee on Jail Reforms 1980-83 deliberated on this problem and observed, "women offenders in India face peculiar problems of rehabilitation during their post-release period. Indian social customs make women ex-prisoners more vulnerable to suspicion and rejection. The stigma of having been in a prison has much more adverse consequences for women than for men. The social system imposes many limitations on them and considers them outcast. They are suppressed and forced to make compromises." Efforts were, however, initiated in the early thirties to set up discharged prisoners' aid societies in various provinces in the country to render assistance and guidance to ex-prisoners for their rehabilitation in the community. But these efforts could not be sustained for want of partronage and community participation.Truly speaking, the institutional treatment programme for prisoners cannot be succussful unless well-organised after-care services are adequately available.

In view of the present unsatisfactory plight of female prisoners, it is necessary to formulate a National Policy on custodial justice to women as recommended by the National Expert Committee on Women Prisoners. In order to review the implications of the proposed policy, the Committee suggested that a statutory autonomous body should be set up with representatives from each component of the criminal justice system and other disciplines like medicine, psychiatry, law, social work, etc. Since the beginning of this century, commendable efforts have been made to improve the conditions of prisons in the country by setting up committees and working groups and a plethora of recommendations also remain on records. The problem, however, is the problem of implementation of all these recommendations.

THE PROBLEM OF TRAFFICKING

At the beginning of the twentieth century, the League of Nations made commendable efforts to bring into focus the problem of traffic in human beings. India was all along associated with this evdeavour to grapple with the problem of trafficking. When the International Agreement for the Suppression of White Slave Traffic was signed by various countries, India was also a signatory to it. In 1921, the League of Nations initiated further action in this direction and held an International Convention for the Suppression of Immoral Traffic in Women and Children which called for the suppression of brothels and proposed measures to discover and prosecute those engaged in traffic of both sexes and those who procured and enticed women and girls for immoral purposes. India also participated in that convention. As a result, the presidencies of Bengal, Bombay and Madras passed their respective laws for the suppression of immoral traffic. Calcutta brought into force its Suppression of Immoral Traffic Act in 1923 and Madras in 1930. In Bombay, the Prevention of Prostitution Act also came into force in 1923. Similarly, the Nayak Girls Protection Act and the Minor Girls Protection Act were passed in U.P. After the World War II, an International Convention for the Suppression of Immoral Traffic in Women was held in New York in 1950 which called upon each nation to tackle the problem of trafficking by enacting suitable laws. India was a party to this Convention. The then existing legislations on the subject in a few states were neither uniform nor comprehensive.

In those circumstances, it was deemed necessary to have a central law which would secure not only uniformity but it would also be sufficiently deterrent for the purpose. Moreover, the Constitution of India under Article 23 provides for the prohibition of traffic in human beings and mentions that any contravention of this provision shall be an offence punishable under the law. In pursuance of this constitutional provision and an international obligation arising out of the New York Convention, the Government of India enacted the Suppression of Immoral Traffic in Women and Girls Act, 1956. It was enforced throughout the country in 1958. It provided for measures to suppress the traffic, abolish brothels and commercialised vice, i.e., traffic in women and girls for the purpose of prostitution as an organised means of livelihood. This Act was intended to be a supplement to the provisions of the Indian Penal Code in respect of kidnapping, sale, abduction, seduction and wrongful restraint of women and girls. It defined the terms 'brothel', 'prostitute', 'prostitution', 'girls', 'protective home' and 'corrective institutions' and provided punishment for keeping a brothel or allowing premises to be used as brothels. It also provided for the setting up of protective homes and corrective institutions for the care, protection, treatment, education, training and rehabilitation of women and girls rescued from the vice.

At present, there are 93 protective/rescue homes and allied institutions in the country with a capacity for 6284* inmates are imparted general education and training in crafts in these homes and are subjected to such disciplinary and moral influences as are likely to promote the prospects of their reformation and rehabilitation. The Second United Nations Seminar on the Prevention of Crime and the Treatment of Offenders, held in Tokyo in 1957 also observed that the problem of prostitution in Asia and the Far East is closely connected with the general level of living as well as with the status of women, and concluded that measures to raise the level of living and the programme directed to raising the status of women to a par with that of man will continue considerably towards decreasing prostitution. With these objectives in view, the institutional care programme was sought to be modernised and equipped with suitable educational and vocational training courses. Subsequently, the success of the after-care

*Source: Quarterly journal Social Defence Vol. XXIX No. 100, April 1990.

programme depends to a large extent on the care taken and training imparted to inmates in institutions.

The Suppression of Immoral Traffic in Women and Girls Act, 1956 was amended in 1978 to make it more effective. It was again amended in 1986. As a result of this amendment, the title of the Act has been changed from "Suppression of Immoral Traffic in Women and Girls Act" to "Immoral Traffic (Prevention) Act" and for the words "Women and Girls" and "Woman and Girl" wherever they occur in the Act, the words 'persons' and 'person' have respectively been substituted. Now the Act prohibits traffic in human beings and not traffic in women and girls only. Under the amended Act the emphasis is on the prevention of immoral traffic as opposed to the original act where the emphasis was on suppression of immoral traffic. The main amendments are as under:

i) The name of the Act is now the Immoral Traffic (Prevention) Act;

ii) penalties for offences involving children and minors have been made more stringent by enhancing the period of imprisonment;

iii) trafficking police officers have been provided under the Act to investigate offences with inter-state ramifications;

iv) licensing authorities have been empowered to suspend licences of hotels where children or minors are detained to be exploited for purposes of prostitution;

v) in cases of seduction in custody, the punishment has been enhanced to that laid down for rape in the Indian Penal Code;

vi) the facility of release of convicted persons on probation of good conduct or after due admonition, etc., has been done away with.

vii) provision has been made for medical examination of all persons removed from a brothel after a search;

viii) Women or girls removed from a brothel after a search, shall be interrogated by women police officers or in absence by such police officers they shall be interrogated in presence of a woman social worker;

ix) the Central Government has been empowered to set up special courts with jurisdictions to try offences having inter-state ramifications.

Chapter 5

PERILOUS TREND

ALCOHOLISM AND DRUG ABUSE

The problem of alcoholism and drug abuse has now assumed a global proportion. It has adversely affected the individual, family and society. It is, therefore, becoming a matter of serious concern all over the world. In fact, alcohol and drugs were in use even in the remote past. These were mainly used to get relief from pain and misery and to attain a state of forgetfulness. In ancient India, the Aryans used to drink a kind of beverage, called '*Soma Rasa.*' There are also copious instances of the use of addictive drugs in various other countries in the hoary past. There is a legend that both opium and hashish were cast into wine by Helen of Troy to soothe all pain and sorrow. Many Greek and Roman physicians had referred to the medicinal properties of opium. Hippocrates (460-357 B.C.) recommended the juice of the poppy for uterine suffocation. A Chinese surgeon is also said to have administered a narcotic drug called Ma Fu Shuan to his patients before operations. Similarly, there are numerous references to the sleep-producing properties of canabis in the Arabian Nights. It may, therefore, be seen that drugs have been used and misused in different cultures since time immemorial.

The term 'drug abuse' refers to the excessive and unregulated use of drugs. Although these were in use in the traditional society, their use was always controlled within the framework of a community-oriented value system. With the passage of time, the traditional pattern of society has undergone a change with new values and opportunities. As a result, the younger generations have been greatly affected. Ari Kiev (1975) opined that drug abuse referred to a type of maladaptive effort to relieve psychological distress by means of a variety of naturally occurring and manufactured pharmacologically active substances or drugs which alter mood, thought and behaviour. While a propensity to use drugs to alleviate distress is a universal characteristic of human beings, the unmonitored and excessive use of such substances is symptomatic of the combined effects of psychological vulnerability and environmental pressures.

Opium, *ganja* and *bhang* which are of vegetable origin and derived from natural sources were in use in India. However, synthetic drugs like tranquillizers, pathedine and L.S.D. are generally becoming popular among students and younger generations. Opium is either taken in the form of a pill or as a solution of the same in water. It can be taken with milk as well. It is supposed to have a sedative effect in minor digestive disorders. It also helps in relieving cough and pain and producing sleep. Sometimes infants are given opium so that they may keep quiet and allow their mothers to go for their chores. This habit is prevalent mainly in industrial areas.

In course of time, the harmful effects of opium were gradually realised by the people all over the country. It was deemed necessary to take drastic steps to control this evil habit. A high level conference was organised by the Government of India in New Delhi in 1949 which was attended by the concerned ministers of the States. The Conference deliberated on the problem at length and passed a resolution that within a maximum period of ten years, opium should be controlled so that it might be used only for scientific and medicinal purposes. It was also recommended that quasimedical use of opium should be eliminated as early as possible.

The hemp drugs commonly used in India, are all derived from the plant cannabis sativa which grows almost all over the country. *Bhang* is the dried leaf, *ganja* the flowering twig and *charas* the resinous exudate obtained from the cannabis plant. The hemp drugs are the narcotics most extensively used by the poor people throughout the country. Hemp grows wild on extensive tracts in northern India along the slopes of the Himalayas. Dried *bhang* leaves are made into a paste by pounding in stone grinders. The pounded mass is then diluted with water and seasoned with black pepper, sugar, etc. Unlike opium, *ganja* or any other narcotics, drinking of *bhang* leaves has no social stink around the consumer. On the contrary, it is considered as a luxury. The leaves are sometimes chewed raw for their sedative effect and to counteract the strain of long distance travel. On festive occasions, *bhang kachauri* or *bhang laddu* are often prepared. Some other preparations of *bhang* are also prevalent. Sometimes powdered *ganja* is boiled in syrup or jaggery.

Cocaine too as an intoxicant has been in use since long. Cocoa plant does not grow in India. It is said to have been introduced in India from Java sometime between 1890 and 1900. It is believed to have been first used in India at the town of Bhagalpur where some land-lords used this drug for relief of dental pain. Subsequently, the Government imposed restrictions on the use of cocaine.

Drugs are beneficial when used wisely by people. But the abuse of the same drugs spells disaster for individuals, families and society as a whole. It is often cited that drug abuse leads to crimes as a result of reduced impulse control, paranoia and negligence. It also affects the family life, law and order, economic production and human welfare.While analysing the causes of drug addiction in this country, a few factors mainly responsible for the spread of this evil, may be highlighted:

i) Rapid industrialisation and urbanisation have ushered in a new way of life with new values like individualism and permissiveness. As a result, the age-old inhibition, taboos and traditional social control mechanism have ceased to remain in force;
ii) lack of parental control partly due to the working situation of both the parents and the break-up of the joint family system are contributory factors;
iii) in consequence of the recent developments in medical sciences, a variety of potent synthetic substances are produced. This has contributed significantly to drug abuse among the youth;
iv) people often take drugs for relief of painful illness and ultimately become dependent on them;
v) frustration and emotional stravation due to various reasons lead people to associate themselves with addicts and get habituated to drugs;

vi) hippie culture also leads many youngmen to drug addiction;

vii) lack of the knowledge of child psychology and communication gap between parents and young addicts are often contributory factors.

All forms of drug dependence lead to the steady deterioration of the personality. Personal care and habits of an individual deteriorate. Skills and abilities are gradually impaired and life becomes oriented around the drug. What is worse, the addict becomes deceitful and untrustworthy. His ethical sense becomes dull. Drugs gradually drain the strength out and lead to dire consequences. Moreover, the constant use of drugs leads to chronic bronchitis, asthma and sometimes even T.B. Everyone in such a predicament will like to escape from something or the other and get liberated. But it is just the opposite with the addict. He becomes a slave commanded by drugs and ultimately plunges into miserable conditions. Like many other groups with common bonds, the drug addicts also have their own world with a language for communication.

Different countries view the drug problem from different angles. The International Criminal Police Organisation (Interpol) conducted a study in 1970 on drug abuse in different countries which revealed that the use of drugs and psychotropic substances had considerably increased among the young people. Each country strives to deal with this problem effectively. But it has not yet been possible to devise an effective method to eradicate this evil. In Britain, the Inter-departmental committee under the Chairmanship of Lord Brain in its report in 1955 observed that there was a serious rise in drug addiction and that the British system of control had broken down. The World Psychiatric Congress held in Madrid in 1966 deliberated on this problem and observed on the basis of reports from different countries that "a rising tide of all forms of addiction, overwhelming the capacities of authorities to control it and defeating, for the most part, attempts at therapeutic amelioration."

As the problem of drug abuse was gradually rearing its ugly head in India, a National Committee on Drug Addiction was set up by the Government of India in 1976. The Committee evaluated the current prevalence of drug abuse in the total population on the basis of data available from a few studies conducted at the national level. In its opinion, these studies had several methodological flaws and as such the conclusions drawn from them were only tentative. In spite of these limitations, the Committee had drawn the following conclusions:

i) In keeping with the Indian tradition, the proportion of those who never used a drug is very large;
ii) alcohol, opium and cannabis are the main drugs abused;
iii) the proportion of regular users is very small, and that of addicts, smaller still (except for tobacco);
iv) the prevalence of drug abuse is substantially more among males than among females.

The Committee observed that in the absence of any longitudinal studies, it was not possible to get a precise idea of drug abuse in the general population. It had, therefore, suggested that studies covering both urban and rural population in different parts of the country should be undertaken and such studies periodically repeated to assess the trend of drug abuse in the country. Earlier, the Ministry of Social Welfare, Government of India sponsored a multi-disciplinary research project to assess the incidence of drug abuse among students. The study was conducted at three metropolitan centres, viz., Bombay, Delhi and Madras and three non-metropolitan centres, viz., Jaipur, Hyderabad and Jabalpur and one residential university at Varanasi. The results of these studies revealed that an overwhelming percentage of students in all these centres had not taken any drug at all.

The Department of Social Welfare (now Ministry of Welfare) sponsored 11 research studies in 1975-76, which were completed in 1978. Seven of these studies were conducted amongst students in the University centres of Bombay, Delhi, Hyderabad, Jabalpur, Jaipur, Madras and Varanasi. The remaining 4 studies were focussed on rural areas of Punjab, on industrial workers in Delhi and on the 'Dome' community of Varanasi. The findings of 7 research studies conducted amongst students showed that the situation was not so alarming at that time.

Another study was also undertaken in the rural areas of Punjab which revealed that the most commonly abused drugs were alcohol, tobacco and opium. Out of the males who consumed drugs, 58.3% were addicted to alcohol, 19.3% to tobacco, 6.3% to opium and 1.2% to cannabis. Among the females, excluding those below

15 years and unmarried girls, tobacco use was reported in 4.0% cases, followed by alcohol in 1.4%, pain-killers in 0.8%, tranquillisers in 0.5% and opium in 0.4%. Abuse of other drugs was not seen in women. According to the conclusions of the study among the industrial workers in Delhi, Alcohol, *charas*, *bhang*, *ganja* and opium were the main drugs used by them. A large number of workers used drugs to get relief from the strain of working in difficult working conditions in the factories or because of the lack of adequate facilities for recreation. The study also pointed out that a majority of the users (59.7%) took to drugs after they had started their career as industrial workers. All these studies were unanimous in their findings that use of drugs like heroin, pathedine and morphine was almost insignificant. With a view to assessing the magnitude of the problem of drug abuse among various population groups, a number of studies were sponsored by the Ministry of Welfare, Government of India.

India is at present facing the problem of increasing trafficking in drugs. Heroin and hashish are supplied from the Near and Middle East region to the western countries through this subcontinent. As a result of this transit traffic, the major cities like Bombay, Calcutta, Madras and Delhi have become vulnerable to drug trafficking. A large quantity of heroin and hashish was seized in this country in 1986. The narcotic drug statistics for the year 1991* reveal the position in respect of quantities of various drugs seized during the year with no. of cases as under:

Drugs	Quantity	Cases
Opium	2145 kg	566
Morphine	6 kg	21
Heroin	622 kg	1158
Ganja	52633 kg	3140
Hashish	4413 kg	335
Cocaine	0.008 kg	1
Methaqualone	4415	78

While indicating action taken against persons involved in drug trafficking, it has been highlighted that 5393 persons were arrested including 93 foreigners, 5546 persons were prosecuted, 855 were convicted and 1940 were acquitted during the year 1991.

*Source: Crime in India 1991' published by National Crime Records Bureau, M.H.A., Government of India.

Legal measures are necessary to deal with the rising trend of trafficking in drugs. Earlier, there were central laws for the control of drugs, viz., the Opium Act, 1858, the Dangerous Drugs Act, 1930, the Drugs and Cosmetics Act, 1940, the Medicinal and Toilet Preparations Act, 1953 and the Customs Act, 1962. Now the Narcotic Drugs and Psychotropic Substances Act, 1985 has been brought into force all over the country to deal with the problem more effectively. The Act provides for a minimum punishment of 10 years' rigorous imprisonment and a fine of Rs. 1 lakh which may be extended to Rs. 2 lakhs and rigorous imprisonment of 20 years'. In respect of repeat offences, the Act provides for a minimum punishment of 15 years rigorous imprisonment, extendable upto 30 years and also a minimum fine of Rs. 1.5 lakhs which may go up to Rs. 3 lakhs. The courts have been empowered to impose fines exceeding these limits for reasons to be recorded in their judgments. The Central Government has invested officers of Customs and Central Excise, Revenue Intelligence, Narcotics Control Bureau and the like with the powers of an officer-in-charge of a Police Station for investigating drug offences under this Act. The provisions of Conservation of Foreign Exchange Regulation Act are also being invoked for detention of narcotics smugglers, wherever justified. An apex body, "Narcotics Control Bureau" for effectively preventing and combating the abuse of drugs and illicit traffic has been constituted under the new Act. The Bureau has five zonal offices each at Delhi, Bombay, Calcutta, Madras and Varanasi. Separate narcotic cells have been created in all the collectorates of Customs and Central Excise all over the country for exclusively dealing with drug related offences.

An important feature of the new Act relates to the status of the drug addict. The Act lays down, *inter alia* punishment for illegal possession in small quantity for personal consumption of any narcotic drug or psychotropic substance or consumption of such drug or substance. The punishment is for one year's imprisonment or fine or both, or imprisonment of six months or fine or both, under specified circumstances. It further empowers the court to release an addict for undergoing medical treatment for detoxification or deaddiction from a hospital or an institution maintained or recognised by the Governemnt. With this end in view, the Act requires the Government to establish as many centres as it thinks fit for identification, treatment, education, after-care, rehabilitation and social reintegration of addicts.

It is essential to create awareness among people about the horrible consequences of drug addiction. The Ministry of Welfare has, therefore, evolved a comprehensive policy for mobilising voluntary action to create an awareness and consciousness for the prevention of drug abuse. A large number of voluntary organisations are being financially assisted to educate the people about the ill-effects of drug addiction. The Ministry has also given funds for establishment of counselling and deaddiction facilities at various centres. Besides, the State Governements have been requested to assess drug abuse situation in various towns and to draw up an integrated plan of action to tackle the problem in all its dimensions.

The Ministry of Information & Broadcasting has adopted a multi-media approach towards awareness building for drug abuse control. Under the Department of Education, the Ministry of Human Resource Development had set up a committee to go into the question of drug addiction in the universities and to make appropriate recommendations. The University Grants Commission also circulated among all the universities a proposal regarding the establishment of counselling and guidance centres in educational institutions as part of the overall programme of students' welfare. A United Nations Mission headed by the Assistant Secretary General and Executive Director of the UN Fund for Drug Abuse Control visited India in October 1986. The aim of the Mission was to explore the possibility of increasing cooperation between UNFEDAC and Government of India in developing on-going programmes for drug abuse prevention. The meeting of the Technical Committee on the prevention of Drug Trafficking and Drug Abuse constituted by the South Asian Association for Regional Cooperation was held from April 12 to 15, 1987 in Islamabad, Pakistan. The meeting arrived at a number of important conclusions recommending, *inter alia*, greater cooperation among SAARC Member countries in controlling drug trafficking and drug abuse.

The Ministry of Welfare functions as the nodal Ministry for the prevention of drug abuse and the rehabilitation of drug addicts. Further, the Ministry of Health and Family Welfare is directly concerned with the treatment aspect of the problem and it has initiated activities both on long term and short term basis to deal with this problem. In January, 1986, an Expert Committee on Drug De-addiction was set up by it to look into the facilities for the treatment of drug addicts and to suggest improvement in the future perspective. In its report submitted in July 1986, the Committee suggested that a National centre should be established to deal with all aspects of research, treatment, manpower development, health services delivery and drug abuse monitoring and prevention in the country, with similar centres at the State level.

In view of the socio-cultural and economic conditions of the country, voluntary treatment is preferable to compulsory treatment under the law. A comprehensive scheme has, therefore, been initiated by the Ministry of Welfare for the setting up of commumity-based counselling and guidance, de-addiction and rehabilitation centres. Under this scheme, seven counselling and guidance centres were established in Delhi under the voluntary sector. These centres deal with various aspects of the problem such as identification, provision of rehabilitation cover, supply of information regarding the sources of treatment, coordination with other rehabilitation agencies, data collection and storage, dissemination of knowledge, liaison with enforcement agencies and psychological aid by way of individual and group therapy.

As a matter of fact, drug addiction is a psycho-socio-medical problem and as such the entire life situation of the addict is to be taken into consideration for the purpose of treatment. Treatment needs to be individualised in each case, keeping in view the distinct personality traits of the addict, nature and degree of addiction and the circumstances in which it occurs. For durable effectiveness, the treatment process should include all the medical, psychological and social aspects of the problem and there should be a multi-disciplinary team of experts working in close liaison with the family members of the addict aided by law enforcement and welfare agencies. Alcoholism and drug addiction is an illness by which the whole family or the group to which the addict belongs are affected and as such, all the aspects of his life relating to or affecting his personality are to be dealt with for a successful and lasting treatment and rehabilitation programme, which will retrieve such persons and restore them to society as useful citizens.

GAMBLING

Gambling is a powerful source of crime. It is an ancient evil. It is a form of crime in which the victims are willing accomplices. The ancient books and epics contain references to gambling. The *Rigveda* contains a hymn highlighting the deplorable plight of a gambler. The *Atharvaveda* also makes a mention of gambling. In the *Mahabharata*, Yudhisthira played dice when he was challenged to it and had to undergo untold sufferings and tribulations. Thus, the great epic depicts the miserable consequences of gambling as a reprehensible pastime. Those who indulge in it, lose all sense of duty, morality, love and affection and often devise ingenious means for securing money for gambling. Peterson (1947) contends that gambling is an important factor contributing to embazzlement. The *Puranas* also emphatically denounce it and highlight the fact that the gambler's wife is always in distress and the gambler plunges himself and his family in endless miseries. Similarly, Manu disapproved gambling. He called upon the King to suppress gambling as it was ruinous and degrading. According to him, it was open theft which should be ruthlessly put down by the king in the interest of the State.

Gambling involves any risk-taking activity. It can, therefore, be defined as a bet on the outcome of a probability game. Those who participate in such games, do so voluntarily. Fun, excitement and occasional thrill of winning fabulous amounts often motivate them. In fact, it is a sport which is carried on with inanimate objects such as dice, pieces of leather, ivory and the like in which there is a stake. It is also carried on with animate objects such as cocks, pigeons, rams, buffaloes and wrestlers.

Marvin Zuckerman opines that those who search out high sensation, have a biological need for it. Some psychologists even go to the length of saying that gambling can be psychologically beneficial. They compare the excitement of gambling to the intoxication of drugs. It becomes well-nigh impossible for a gambler to resist the will of indulging in the risk taking activity. A compulsive gambler continues to bet because the action becomes a source of forgetting the outside world replete with multifarious problems. His anxieties associated with his wife, family, debts or job disappear when he concentrates on money and action (Livingston). Affluent gamblers are not generally affected much by gambling losses. But heavy gambling with continuous losses may spell disaster for the individual and his family. It leads to personal maladjustment and often mental derangement. Although it is regarded as a sport and a source of relaxation, it is wasteful, unproductive and anti-social.

In the days of yore, English noblemen used to gamble as a regular pastime. It was customary for an English nobleman to know how to play cards or handle dice. To deal with this problem, the Puritans enacted a legislation in 1657 which provided that losers in gambling transactions could sue for the recovery of twice the sum lost. Thereafter, it was decided to protect the land aristocracy of England from the consequences of excessive gambling. In 1710, the Gambling Act was passed in England. In course of time, some gambling activities like horse racing were legalised. Lotteries have gradually become popular as they provide an opportunity to amass huge wealth by sheer luck.

Of late, many States and Union Territory Administrations in India have introduced State lotteries. These lotteries are justified on the ground that they lead to economic activities and help in capital formation and are not wasteful as in other risk-taking games. However, the fact remains that the rewards of gambling are distributed on the basis of chance and as such it makes a mockery of the legitimate economy with its stress on rationality, discipline and hard work. In gambling situations, there are unrealistic aspirations and an environment of uncertainty. A belief in luck may help in encouraging risk assumption, but excessive reliance on luck leads to lack of efforts, initiative and action.

The subject of gambling falls under List II-State List, entry 34 of the Constitution of India. Different States and Union Territories have their respective laws governing gambling and betting. Statistics available from the "Crime in India", 1991 published by the National Crime Records Bureau, Ministry of Home Affairs, Government of India reveal that 3,68,920 persons were arrested under the Gambling Acts of various States during 1991 as against 3,69,530 persons in 1990.

The highest number of cases (93,883) under these Acts was recorded by Maharashtra followed by Madhya Pradesh (59,314), Tamil Nadu (39,927), Gujarat (39,229), Andhra Pradesh (36,007), Uttar Pradesh (30,600), West Bengal (17,778) and Karnataka (17,252). Among the Union Territories, the highest number of cases under the Gambling Acts was registered in Delhi (6,206) followed by Pondicherry (339) and Chandigarh (294). Similarly, among the metropolitan cities, the maximum number of cases under the Gambling Acts was registered in Bombay (38,385) followed by Calcutta (16,423), Madras (5,126), Ahmedabad (15,392), Delhi (6,013) and Nagpur (6,059). However, these statistics may not reflect the exact magnitude of the problem of gambling as quite a number of such cases evade the notice of the law enforcement agencies and ultimately legal action. In some remote rural areas and even in urban slums, gamblers carry on their nefarious activities without any hindrance. Lure of easy money, lack of proper recreational facilities, unemployment and underemployment are some of the important causes of gambling.

Legal action alone cannot eradicate or deal with this problem. It is necessary to involve the community in any programme of social action. Organised recreational facilities, religious discourses, production-cum-training centres, etc., are required at vulnerable places to provide constructive leisure-time activities for those who are prone to such anti-social tendencies.

CORRUPTION

There are different types of criminal behaviour in our society. One such behaviour is corruption. It can be broadly defined as an act inimical to the interest of society. It impairs the moral fabric of society and hampers the normal social processes and involves an intentional disregard of law from improper motives and as such, it is something against law—a vicious and fraudulent intention to evade the prohibitions of the law. In almost all developing countries, corruption is a serious problem which stands in the way of socio-economic development. It takes different forms and penetrates into every sphere of life. Thus, we find corruption in politics, in administration, in business, in education and even in religion. It may be in the form of a minor favour done out of turn to facilitate the work of an individual. It may also take the form of a major irregularity committed to enhance the interests and prospects of an individual. Sometimes corruption may lead to harassment and extortion in an attempt to seek gratification for one's personal ends. However, in almost all cases of corruption, there is blatant misuse of authority which is generally derived from office—political, governmental, industrial, educational and religious. There are also traditional and charismatic forms of authority. For example, Gurus live luxurious lives at the expense of their credulous disciples.

In order to gain insight into the problem of corruption, it is necessary to understand the social milieu of a country. In fact, the social conditon in this country is complex. The caste system with various religious sects automatically creates a psychological inequality and gives rise to the problem of a lack of social cohesion. Thus we often come across primordial group affiliations of caste or religion. Economically the people are generally poor with subsistence or below subsistence levels of income. There is, or course, a small section of people like landlords, industrialists, business magnets, professionals, bureaurcrats, etc., who are quite well-off. There are also middle income group people who are neither very well-off nor are they at the abject poverty level. So, there is a glaring economic inequality among the people.

At the educational level, there is a large illiterate population in the country. There are also school educated and college educated population. The majority of these people live in urban areas with a propensity for Western ideas and modernity. Therefore, there is a yawning gulf between these sections of people and the illiterate rural masses with the age-old traditional ideas.

In a democracy like India, the principle of equality is valid only in the exercise of franchise. But in this sphere also equality does not prevail if individuals are guided by primordial group affiliations of caste, community and religion. Such factors often lead to chaos and confusion and it becomes well-nigh impossible for the people to exercise their voting rights freely and rationally. Allurement, force and at times rigging work the election scenario in this country. Even at the post-election stage, floor crossing in contravention of the Anti-defection law takes place. It is a usual practice to wean elected members by a party to augment its group strength at the political level. In such unfavourable conditions, democratic functioning can not be satisfactory and fails to achieve the aspirations of the people in the long run.

For proper democratic functioning, there is need for open and free elections in which different political parties and individuals endeavour to wean the electoate to secure a majority and a mandate to shoulder the yoke of administration of the country. Truly speaking, votes in such elections lie in the hands of a predominently poor electorate. Different political parties avail themselves of the opportunity to hold out high hopes of their respective election manifestos for ameliorating the deplorable conditions of the masses. At the same time, the parties need enormous amounts of money to defray the election expenses. If a party contests all the seats to the Parliament and the State legislatures, huge amounts of money are required. The party cannot raise as much funds from its own resources. So it has to look to other sources of funds which are clandestinely made available to it by the well-to-do sections of society for the purpose of fighting the elections.

The law provides for the prevention of such practices by limiting the expenditure that may be incurred by each candidate on his election work, viz., printing of posters, support of volunteers, organising meeting at various places, travel through the constituency, etc. Thus, theoretically the declared election expenditure of the candidate is limited to the maximum that is specified. But in actual practice, the declared amounts of money are like the tips of icebergs. The vast mass is, therefore, submerged and remain unseen. The enormity of expenditure for election purposes in a poor country like India is beyond anybody's comprehension. The duel policy of an egalitarian slogan and the helpless dependence upon the affluent sections to procure funds for fighting elections generates an atmosphere of hypocrisy in this country. In fact, this hypocrisy is at the root of all evils in our national life.

Those who provide financial support to the dominant party want to be compensated in some ways. Their claims may take the form of convenient price fixation of commodities, variation of licensing policies for imports and exports, redefinition of criteria of eligibility or otherwise for public borrowing or borrowing from public financial institutions. The Govt. is supposed to take decisions in such matters in the public interest, but it can also do so promoting the interest of a particular section of people in response to their pressure. The goal of an ideal welfare State can never be achieved in such unfavourable conditions.

It is really a matter of serious concern that corruption has also spread in education and judicial departments. Mass copying in examination halls at the connivance of invigilators is a common feature at same places. Admission in professional courses becomes difficult for students with meagre resources. A person with low calibre may get admission by paying handsome capitation money. Similarly, by buying witnesses offenders reduce criminal trials to a mockery. They can virtually take the entire control of the administration of justice in their own hands by dint of their capacity to spend and pay the price of witnesses. The currupt can win legal battles by engaging eminent lawyers to defend their cases. Eye witnesses often turn hostile under the influence of the offender or after accepting money from him. As a result, prosecution ultimately fails. This is really a shocking state of affairs. All efforts of the police officers in such matters are thus wasted simply because the accused can purchase some important witnesses and consequently frustruation takes place among the enthusiastic, honest and sincere officers. Nobody, therefore, takes any initiative to unravel the truth and prefers to be swayed by the existing current of time.

There are examples galore of officials with courage and devotion being harassed and put to insurmountable difficulties for taking initiative and interest to unearth mysteries in some cases involving influential persons. In reality, it is often found that the more corrupt a person is, the greater is his influence and position to bring about pressure on officers and various other agencies to see that no effective legal action is taken against him. In such circumstances, social justice so loudly proclaimed by the leaders, can hardly be achieved in this country. In fact, corruption is the result of maladministration and unless administration is set right, all hopes of eradicating this evil will be ulitmately belied. A clean administration and honest citizenry are essential in a country wedded to the ideals of the Welfare State.

Even before independence the evil of corruption started polluting the social atmosphere in the country. The World War II gave a fillip to this unwholesome trend. Enormous expenditure was incurred for purposes connected with the war. It gave rise to a situation which provided unscrupulous and anti-social persons, both officials and non-officials, with opportunities for corrupt practices. After the war also, extensive reconstruction activities offered wide scopes of corrupt practices and the possibility of their continuance in future. So the then Govt. of India realised the necessity to set up an organisation to investigate offences of corruption committed by public servants. Accordingly, the Delhi Police Establishment was set up in 1941 by an executive order of the Central Govt. under the administration of a Deputy Inspector General of Police with the head quarters at Lahore, for the purpose of investigating cases of corruption connected matters relating to the War Department. This special force belonged to the Defence Department which was then called War Department. Subsequently, an ordinance was promulgamated constituting a special police force for the investigation of certain offences committed in connection with the departments of the Central Government. This ordinance was replaced by the Delhi Special Police Establishment Ordinance in 1946. Later on, it became the Delhi Special Police Establishment Act with the jurisdiction to cover all the departments of the Government of India. Now it extends to all the States and Union Territories.

After the Second World War, the Prevention of Corruption Act was passed in 1947. It was highlighted in the statement of Objects and Reasons of this Bill that "the scope for bribery and corruption of public servants had been enormously increased by war conditions and though the war is now over, opportunities for corrupt practices will remain for a considerable time to come." This Act was amended in 1952 and a new section 5A relating to investigation into cases under this Act was incorporated. It now extends to the whole of India except the State of Jammu and Kashmir. Prior to this Act, the offences of bribery and corruption used to be dealt with under the provisions of sections 161 to 165 of the Indian Penal Code. But the offences under these sections were not cognizable.

The provisions of the Prevention of Corruption Act can be utilised against a public servant who has amassed wealth disproportionate to the known sources of income. But the difficulty arises in some cases when nobody comes forward to give evidence against a public servant because of his wealth and influence. Such persons are also in a position to bring about pressure on officers and various other agencies so that no effective legal action is taken against them. Nothing can be done—no remedies can be available when individuals both in high and low positions are corrupt. The recent events like Bofors and the stocks scam are alleged to have involved a considerable nexus between the bureaucracy, the political Government and corrupt business players.

As a matter of fact, corruption has cast a nationwide net which can only be severed by the people trapped beneath it.

Despite the prevailing uncongenial situation, there are some persons of high integrity who discharge their functions with devotion and sincerity overcoming all sorts of allurements. But the number of such persons is gradually dwindling as it is becoming increasingly difficult for them to thrive in an environment riddled with rampant corruption, immorality and dishonesty. It is high time for us to ponder why our standard of morality has abysmally gone down since independence. Some reasons may, however, be adduced for the present reprehensible state of affairs. The alarming increase of population and spiralling prices of essential commodities are important factors in giving rise to the problem of corruption. Some people take recourse to illegal gratification to meet their requirements for their survival.

The age-old value system has undergone a change. Now people have an insatiable desire for power and pelf and this very attitude of people is responsible for many ills in society. The position and status of a person is generally judged from his wealth and how he demonstrates it in his day-to-day life. Nobody bothers whether the wealth is legitimately acquired or not. This value system motivates a person to attain social status by any means. Therefore, indiscipline, insincerity and selfishness have permeated the entire atmosphere. There is no paucity of surmons and preachings by the people in power. But the fact remains that people are more impressed by what is practised than by what is proclaimed as a precept. People are generally imitative.

The Constitutional guarantee of 'equality before law' is only on records. In reality, money power counts and even a culprit can get away with impunity by dint of his financial resources and influence in the community while a poor man suffers irreparably. It is often found that poor offenders are taken in custody on flimsy grounds and languish there for months and even for years together. Nobody comes to their rescue because they are unable to spend money. So justice becomes a far cry for them.

Passive attitude of the people is also responsible for the increasing trend of corruption in this country. The people remain silent and tolerate injustice, illegality, and wrong action done in front of them. They cannot come together to oppose any adverse trend in society. There are very few people who think in terms of the community. Once their self-interest is achieved, they hardly care for the common interest. Truly speaking, the people's sense of moral outrage seems to have been bludgeoned into passivity.

While discussing the measures to deal with the problem of corruption, the examples of some developed and more advanced countries may also be cited. The bribery of judges was a serious problem in Egypt and Babylonia. In the fifth Century B.C. bribery of Greek officials by foreign powers was common. Simultaneously, corruption increased by leaps and bounds due to the accelerated economic activities and the political insensibility to the problem. As a result, the people lost their interest in the government. Similarly, in Rome bribery was common in public elections, in the senate, and in the courts. In England also, corrupt practices were prevalent even in the common law courts. The institution of the Chancellorship could not provide adequate remedy for the injustices of the common law courts there. In France, during the fifteenth century the evil practice of the sale of judicial offices was in vogue. Other countries like Spain and Portugal had also similar problems. The colonial governors of these countries amassed huge wealth through their absolute power over colonies far removed from the Central Government which were interested in the colonies as a source of revenue only.

In India, the officials of the British East India Company indulged in a variety of venal practices and enriched themselves. Even in Japan, the naval scandals of 1914, the bribery of members of Parliament during the second OKuma Ministry and the corrupt election practices which could not be stopped by the Act of 1901, are all proofs of the existence of corruption at that time. The situation was even worse in China. However, in Russia there was a tremendous improvement in official morality under the then communist Government. The crusading zeal of the party in power could bring about a reform in administration by inflicting severe punishment on all corrupt officials. These violent measures, of course, produce dazzling results for a particular period only. Therefore, for a long-term remedial measure there should be a non-pecuniary system of values and people should develop a permanently heightened sense of community service. There are countries like Switzerland and England which could get rid of the evil of corruption without violence. As a matter of fact, no particular type of government can provide a guarantee against corruption.

Even the Pappacy and Theocratic States like the Hedrew State were not free from corruption.

Although corruption existed in some advanced countries in the past, it has now almost disappeared from the civil service of these countries. They have developed the civil service with adequate salaries and permanent tenure and a professional code of ethics has also been developed among the civil servants. Moreover, Government bodies for the specific purpose of detecting inefficiency and corruption have been set up to tackle this problem. As a result, an important source of corruption has been removed.

The developing countries like India where progress of developmental activities has been hampered to a considerable extent due to rampant corruption, may take a cue from the advanced countries which have been able to do away this evil and strive to deal with the problem more effectively. Venality can be eliminated only when those at the helms of affairs and the people in general sincerely intend to do so. On the whole, political apathy, indifference of the people with money-minded culture which values all things in terms of money, are factors mainly responsible for the existence of corruption in this country.

The statistics for the year 1990 available from "Crime in India" published by the National Crime Records Bureau, Ministry of Home Affairs reveal that 1338 persons were arrested under the Prevention of Corruption Act and related sections of the Indian Penal Code during the year 1990 and 174 and 216 were ultimately convicted in 1990 and 1991 respectively. However, the alarming problem of the large-scale corruption can not be gauged from these figures. It is, therefore, necessary to make concerted efforts in launching a tirade against corruption. For this purpose all sections of people, particularly the youth should be awakened and enthused to strike at the root of this problem which has been eating into the vitals of the nation. All modes of publicity media should be utilised to educate the people on this social scourge through the length and breadth of the country. Citizens' Councils at various levels may be very useful to ensure community participation for this lofty purpose. In fine, the words of the *Upanishada* may be recalled in this connection—" Arise, awake and stop not till the goal is reached."

TERRORISM

The word 'terrorism' means the use of force and violence to intimidate or to subjugate a particular section of people or Government. Similarly, the word 'terror' is used in Latin 'to frighten'. Thus, 'terrorist' is defined as a person causing intense fear and terribleness. In Webster's International Dictionary the expression 'terrorism' is defined as 'systematic use of terror as a means of coercion.' The Oxford English Dictionary defines it as a political term connected with revolutionary activities. However, terrorism is not a mass movement but it is carried out by small groups of people. The Terrorist and Disruptive Activities (Prevention) Act, 1987 defines 'terrorist' as a person who indulges in wanton killing of persons or in violence or in the disruption of service or means of communications essential to the community or in damaging property with a view to: (1) putting the public or any section of the public in fear; or (2) affecting adversely the harmony between different religious, racial, language or regional gorups or castes or communities; or (3) coercing or overawing the Government established by law; or (4) endangering the sovereignty and integrity of India.

Terrorism is a global problem and it has been practised through the ages. The ancient Greek historian Xenophon wrote of the effectiveness of psychological warfare against enemy populations. The Roman emperors like Tiberius and Calligula used banishment, expropriation of property and execution as means to discourage opposition to their rule. The Spanish Inquisition used arbitrary arrest, torture and execution to punish religious heresy. Robespierre of France used terror as a means of promoting revolutionary ideas paving the way for his political dominance. Likewise, after the civil war in the United States, the defiant Southerners formed a terrorist organisation which was known as the Ku Kolux Klan to intimidate supporters of reconstructions. In the latter half of the 19th century, terrorism reared its ugly head in Western Europe and Russia as well. The idea gained ground that the best way to bring about revolutionary political and social changes was to exterminate the persons in positions of power.

Subsequent technological advances such as automatic weapons and electronic explosives gave a fillip to terrorist activities in the 20th century. Terrorism was also practised by some totalitarian regimes like Nazi Germany under Adolf Hitler and the Soviet Union under Josef Stalin. In these States, arrest, imprisonment, torture, and execution were carried on with a view to creating a climate of fear and compelling people to abide by the declared policy of the State. Terrorism had also been used in Malaysia, Indonesia, Philippines, Iran, Nicaragua, El Salvador and Argentina in internal conflicts between revolutionary forces and established governments. There was an upsurge of terrorism in 1974 in Italy, Spain and Turkey. In Italy, the then politician Aldo Movo was abducted and subsiquently murdered. In some other countries also, terrorist gangs sprang up, e.g., The Baader-Meinhof gang of West Germany, The Japanese Red Army, Italy's Red Brigades, the Puerto Rican FALN, Al-Fatah and other Palestinian organisations. In India, terrorism took an ugly turn in Kashmir and Punjab and a number of innocent people became victims of the diabolical designs of terrorists.

Earlier, some nationalist groups in India employed terrorist methodology in their struggle against the alien rule. But those activities were basically different from contemporary terrorism as much of the violence at that time was directed against the foreign ruler. The political goal of such violence was independence—driving out the Britishers and establishment of a free nation. As a result, there was several assassinations by political terrorists. The Chapekar Association in Maharashtra killed a number of British officers in Pune. After the partition of Bengal in 1905, many officers were done to death, especially in Calcutta. Police stations and armouries were raided. The Chittagong armoury was raided in 1930. In truth, terrorism was employed during that period to assert the country's self-respect against the foreign rule. None of those Indian terrorists was, however, able to overshadow the tremendously popular non-violence movement initiated by Mahatma Gandhi. As a matter of fact, terrorism does not require public support which is essential in launching a vigorous national struggle. It has also to be differentiated from insurgency. An insurgent has the support of a large section of people while a terrorist need not have such support. Moreover, an insurgent is a national of a country who rises in revolt against the Government of his country and fights to overthrow the same by guerilla warfare. On the contrary, the terrorist may or may not be a national of the country in which he operates. The worst aspect of terrorism is that it often cruelly hits those who are innocent and not in any way responsible for any injustice.

All efforts to combat terrorism have so far proved to be ineffective. The reason is not very far to seek. No country appears to have understood and appreciated the underlying causes of terrorism. One of the important causes of terrorism is injustice against a particular group. The examples of Roman Catholics in Ireland and the Palestinians who suffered from historical injustices may be cited in this connection. The young man is generally averse to accept the inevitable frustration involved in growing up. He is confronted with the discrepancy between the ideals he cherishes and the ugly realities. It becomes too much for him. In course of time, he develops a disturbed relationship with those in authority and a growing conflict in his mind. As a result, he drifts towards terrorism. The young impressionable mind is also susceptible to various allurements held out by unscrupulous groups of people to achieve their nefarious ends. Adequate finances, technical know-how and other necessary facilities are clandestiney made available to the volatile groups of young people from outside the country and countries like India become an undeclared battle-ground for international terrorism. Repeated hijacking of planes, kidnapping and series of bomb blasts continue.

The problem has, of late, assumed a formidable proportion with the availability of sophisticated arms and ammunition. The present mass-media like T.V. has also played an important role in focussing violence and terrorism. Various events of violence and terrorism are directly brought into millions of houses and viewers irrespective of the old and the young, who are exposed to the terrorists' demands, grievances and political goals. Violence is often glamorised through popular films. In such conditions, the youth in particular gradually become prone to violence and seek to substitute violent acts for legitimate political activities. Sometimes persons suffering from individual insurmountable problems, transfer them on society and seek the solution of these problems through violent action. Accordingly, terrorists attack defenceless targets such as prominent individuals, office buildings, public institutions, business centres and banks. The main objective is to strike terror in people's minds. They continue their destructive activities in order to sustain the fear all around the area of their operation.

While dwelling upon the feasibility of dealing with the problem of terrorism, it should be borne in mind that potential terrorists always exist but a variety of factors determine to a large extent whether they will swing into terrorist action. These factors include *inter alia* cohesion of society, strength and firmness of the State and the general political situation. If all these factors are favourable in a country, terrorism is not likely to thrive. It is a multi-dimensional problem. Therefore, any strategy to combat terrorism has to be multi-dimensional. Both national and international measures are required to grapple with this problem. Different measures are necessary to deal with different kinds of terrorism at the global level. However, it can be effectively tackled by removing some root causes, i.e., (1) by persuading the terrorists to come to the negotiating table; (2) by bringing the misguided youths into the main stream of life; (3) by isolating the extremists; (4) by eliminating differences in perceptions; (5) by sensitising the democratic process; (6) by counselling at the initial stage of terrorist activities.

A number of countries have adopted anti-terrorist measures. The United States of America maintains special military forces with counter-terrorist capabilities. These forces are also well-equipped to carry out rescue operations. Other countries that have counter-terrorist command units are Britain, France, Switzerland, Belgium, Denmark, Italy, The Netherlands, Norway, Austria and Indonesia. There is also one such unit in the British Colony of Hongkong. Some of these countries have jointly made efforts to pool resources to fight the rising trend of terrorism. Actually, any country's programme of action against terrorism must be based on international arrangement to combat this problem across borders making use of extradition agreements and elimination of safe havens, multilateral controls on the transfer of areas and ammunition and agreements for technical assistance and exchange of intelligence. In addition, there should be on-going research programme at the international level to conduct in-depth studies on the problem of terrorism which is gradually assuming an alarming proportion. In this connection, action should also be taken to improve a meaningful international cooperation in respect of security, rescue and anti-terrorist measures.

One of the important anti-terrorist measures is to reduce the finance at the disposal of terrorists. If their finances dwindle, the scale of their operations will automatically be reduced. Of course, it will be well-nigh impossible if a foreign Government clandestinely extends its help to the terrorist group and incite them to continue their depredations. As things stand at present, terrorists take to their heels after perpetrating wanton destructions and take shelter in a neighbouring country. It becomes difficult to trace them out. The recent spate of bomb blasts in Bombay took a heavy toll of human lives and valuable properties. The alleged culprits, Memon Brothers, were reported to have left India to evade action under the law. India is confronted with abominable narco-terrorism which is funded by illegitimate profit from narcotics smuggling. In order to keep track of terrorists and to inflict deterrent punishment on them, an exhaustive system at the international level may be evolved for recording and storing of information about terrorists, their associates, their modus operandi and their sources of finance.

Every State irrespective of its form of Government has to be equipped with the power to punish those who, by their conduct jeopardise the safety and stability of the State through disruptive activities. The Terrorist and Disruptive Activities (Prevention) Act 1987 was enacted to make special provisions for the prevention of, and for coping with terrorist and disruptive activities and for matters connected therewith or incidental thereto. In addition to this Act, there are other Acts which have specific provisions for the prevention of anti-social and disruptive activities, e.g.; the Explosives Act, 1884, the Indian Telegraph Act, 1885, the Indian Railways Act, 1890, the Explosive Substances Act, 1908, the Arms Act, 1959, the Unlawful Activities (Prevention) Act, 1967, the Anti-Hijacking Act, 1982, the Suppression of Unlawful Act Against Safety of Civil Aviation Act, 1982, and the Prevention of Damage to Public Property Act, 1984.

The Terrorist and Disruptive Activities (Prevention) Act, 1987 extends to the whole of India. By virtue of the provisions of sub-section (2) of section I of the Act, the citizens of India outside India and all persons on ships and aircraft registered in India, wherever they may be, are covered. Sub-section (1) of section 3 of the Act defines a terrorist act and provides that whoever with intent to overawe the Government as by law established or to strike terror in the people or any section of the people or to alienate any section of the people or to adversely affect the

like, Andhra Pradesh, Assam, Bihar, Gujarat, Jammu and Kashmir, Karnataka, Maharashtra, Tamil Nadu and West Bengal have their respective laws for detaining a person if his activities are prejudicial to the security of the State or the maintenance of public order, e.g., (1) The Andhra Pradesh Prevention of Dangerous Activities of Bootleggers, Dacoits, Drug Offenders, Goondas, Immoral Traffic Offenders and Land Grabbers Act, 1986, (2) The Assam Preventive Detention Act, 1980, (3) The Bihar Control of Crimes Act, 1981, (4) The Gujarat Prvention of Anti-social Activities Act, 1985, (5) The Jammu and Kashmir Public Safety Act, 1978, (6) The Karnataka Prevention of Dangerous Activities of Bootleggers, Drug-offenders, Gamblers, Goondas, Immoral Traffic Offenders and Slum-Grabbers Act, 1985, (7) The Maharashtra Prevention of Communal, Anti-social and other Dangerous Activities Act, 1980, (8) The Tamil Nadu Prevention of Dangerous Activities of Bootleggers, Drug-offenders, Forest offenders, Goondas, Immoral Traffic offenders and Slum Grabbers Act, 1982.

It transpires from the above discussions that there is a plethora of laws for the prevention of terrorist activities in the country. However, the fact remains that in spite of all these legal measures terrorism continues unabated. Even in Britain with an experienced staff, sensitive intelligence service, highly skilled police force, and public help, terrorism could not be contained. From Northern Ireland it spread to the main land leading to some horrndous crimes. In the U.S. also, the strategy to deal with terrorism included the air-strike against Libya, the arms-for hostages deal with Iran, and many diplomatic and economic sanctions against the sponsors of terrorism. But all these strategies failed to fight terrorism in that country. The failure of these countries to effectively combat terrorism suggests that none has been able to delve deep into its causes and as a result, no permanent remedy is yet in sight.

Chapter 6

POPULATION

POPULATION EXPLOSION

Of late, the problem of population growth has assumed a formidable proportion. India today ranks second in the world in population and seventh in land area. She has about 16 per cent of the world's population on 2.4 per cent of the world's land area. Although she is only about two-fifths the size of the United States, she has about two and a half times the United State's population. The population of undivided India was about 130 million in 1600 A.D. During the following two and a half centuries, the population was about 150 million. Thus, there was only an increase of 20 million during this period due to political instability, famines and epidemics resulting in heavy mortalities. However, with the establishment of the British rule, the restoration of internal peace and the setting up of health and medical services, the population began to grow slowly upto the turn of the 20th century and after 1921, it increased rapidly. According to the first Census of India in 1871-72, the population of India was 206 million. In 1881, the second Census revealed a population of 256 million which decreased by 20 million in 1891. However, it again increased to 251 million in the year 1921. It further indicated that there was an increase of 15 million only in 30 years because of natural calamities like famines, epidemics, pestilence, etc. During the 30 years from 1921 to 1951, the population increased by 110 million and in the decade 1951–61, the population again increased by 78.1 million, which was more than the entire population of any country in Europe with the exception of erstwhile Soviet Union. The present population of India stands at 843,930,861 of which

437,597,929 are males and 406,332,932 females as compared to 683,329,097 in 1981. Thus, the population of India has increased by 160.6 million during the last decade, an addition almost equal to the population added during the three decades from 1931 to 1961. It is, in fact, more than the total population of Japan. The Census reports also bring into focus the fact that India's population has grown steadily during the present century. It further reveals that the density of population was 267 persons per sq. km. in 1991 as against 216 in 1981. The immediate impact of this voluminous population had been the increased pressure on land.

Now the question arises as to what are the factors behind this alarming increase? An explanation may be found in the nation's relatively high birth rate and rapidly declining death rate. There are various reasons as to why India's birth-rate continues to be high despite the deplorable plight of the people in general. In India, everyone sooner or later gets married. Marriage is not merely a necessary institution but a quasi-religious duty. An individual's economic security or emotional maturity are seldom taken into consideration for marriage. There is no individual choice generally in obtaining a husband or a wife. So there is no economic or emotional deterrence to marriage. Even now, in some communities in rural areas children are married before they attain puberty. There are very few men or women who remain without marriage. Almost every adult male and female in the country participates in reproduction. Although sixty years have already elapsed since the Child Marriage Restraint Act (The Sarda Act, 1929), millions of girls are still married early.

In rural areas, a sizable population of teenagers are married who are below the age of consent. It was estimated that the mean age at marriage of females of all religions in India was 15.6 years according to the Census of 1951. However, in the past, an obscurantist feature of the Hindu social customs, i.e. the ban on widow remarriage introduced some relief from the population pressure. There are about 25 million widows of all ages who normally do not marry. Even widowers are generally reluctant to marry widows. The Hindu Widow Remarriage Act was passed in 1856 as a result of the relentless efforts of the renowned social reformer of Bengal Iswar Chandra Vidyasagar who first highlighted the importance of introducing the widow remarriage system in Hindu society. Unfortunately, the social ban against widow remarriage still continues to operate even after more than a century. Of course, in the changing social milieu, there are people who come forward to marry eligible and unencumbered widows. The modern trend is gradually veering in favour of discarding the traditional custom of banning widow remarriage. Thus, some widows also now participate in reproduction and contribute their share to the population growth.

The average Indian wants sons. This attitude becomes very strong in a country like India where there is neither social security nor old age pensions, sickness benefits nor employment insurance for an overwhelming majority of people. Parents have to depend on gainfully employed adult sons for support in their old age. Sons are needed to work in fields, graze cattle, help their parents in numerous other ways and give protection to the family in case of family feuds in the community. Even now, a mother gains social status by the number of sons she bears. Moreover, the continuance of the lineage is of great significance to the people in this country. The *Hindu Dharmasastras* envisage the necessity of at least one son for every Hindu without which the objective of marriage remains unfulfilled. According to Manu, a man proceeds downwards and fails to attain *moksha* without begetting a son. There is a conviction among the Hindus that a sonless person remains indebted to his ancestors. Prompted by these religious beliefs, Hindus are inclined to have larger families.

The Census statistics reveal an interesting and significant phenomenon. The rate of growth among some minority religious groups is consistently higher when compared with that of the majority community or of the nation as a whole. This trend suggests that the members of these groups suffer from the apprehension of their minority status and will consciously or unconsciously attempt to improve their status by enlarging families. It may also be mentioned that the programme of family planning and population control has also suffered on account of political factors. Not a single political party has ever raised its voice against the alarming growth of population in the country and suggested any effective measure to bring down the birth rate. None has spelt out in its manifesto the paramount importance of family planning without which the country will be doomed for all time to come. As a matter of fact, on this issue a national consensus is necessary and every party should support it. Only then, the family planning programme can make any dent in this country. But such a possibility appears to be slim in the present political doldrums.

Furthermore, there is a lack of any effective widespread family planning habit among the rural people who constitute about 70 per cent of India's total population. Birth control measures are of recent origin even in cities, let alone rural areas. One of the factors behind the growth of population is the decline in the nation's death rate. There has been a decline in the infant mortality and the maternal mortality rates due to the improvement of medical facilities, such as an increase in trained medical and paramedical personnel, B.C.G. vaccination for tuberculosis, services of trained midwives, dissemination of health education, foreign technical aid, assistance from the World Health Organisation, etc.

However, India's population needs improvement. It is necessary to reduce the incidence of blindness, deafness, imbecility and various types of mental illness. Every infant has the right to be born healthy. It must be fed, nourished and given the requisite means for its normal development. To achieve this goal, the standard of living of the people is to be raised in terms of the basic requisites of civilised human existence like food, clothing, housing, educational opportunities, health facilities, leisure and cultural amenities. Although the standard of living in general, even in rural areas has improved since independence, it is still far from being satisfactory. The plight of the average man is miserable and distressing. The basic minimum of goods and services for healthy and purposeful living is not adequately available.

The most desirable size of population of a country should be one which permits the maximum production, the highest standard of living, economic security and adequate freedom and leisure for the pursuit of cultural values. Thus, there is an optimum size of population for every country under a particular economic and political system. In India, the greatest obstacle in the path of economic development is the alarming rate of population growth and the low level of living of an overwhelming majority of the people. Her natural resources,. capital, and technological know-how are miserably limited in relation to the magnitude of the problem. The total land area and the natural resources cannot be augmented in keeping with the increasing number of human beings. For solution of all the problems of habitat and food supply, the country has, therefore, to depend on her limited resources.

In fact, food is the biggest problem. A majority of the people suffer from perennial hunger. According to a U.N. survey, four out of every five people in the world have never had and will not have in the foreseeable future what one in America, Canada or Europe take for granted as a good square meal. A majority of the underfed and unfed live in Asia, particularly India. The per capita daily consumption in terms of calories is about 2000 in India as against an estimated minimum requirement of 2300 to 2500 calories. The present low consumption of about 2000 calories in India is in striking contrast to the 3000-3400 calories consumed in the U.S.A., Canada, and the countries in north-west Europe. If the requisite levels of consumption of food both in quality and quantity are taken into consideration, a large number of people in India suffer from serious malnutrition. Good and adequate nutrition not only promotes sound health and reduces morbidity but increase the nation's productivity and promotes overall physical and mental well-being of the people. Nutrition can also serve as an impetus for programmes regulating birth-control as closely spaced and frequent pregnancies in poverty-ridden population is a common cause of maternal malnutrition. There is also a close link between infant nutrition and spacing of births. Thus, nutritional care of mothers and infants as a part of the family planning programme can motivate people to take advantage of this programme.

As regards clothing, the per capita consumption of cotton textiles is miserably low despite the fact that India is a major cotton producing and textile manufacturing country. The housing situation is also not at all satisfactory. A small percentage of the population have housing with certain elementary amenities. The vast majority of the people—almost the entire rural population live in backward and unhygienic hovels without minimum basic amenities. As for urban areas, land has become so scarce and costly and the population pressure so intense in some metropolitan cities that there is tremendous overcrowding with its inevitable consequences of sprawling slums. The problem is all the more accentuated because a part of the existing houses which are in dilapidated conditions, give way due to lack of repair. As things stand at present, even a low cost housing is not feasible to meet the present demands, let alone the provision of housing for the future population. What is worse, a large number of people live on the city pavements for years and generations together. With the increase of population, the problem of housing will be further accentuated and it will be difficult for one to get even a sleeping space in the years to come.

Education is the most important factor which provides the strongest aspiration for better life and amenities and consequent limitation of family size. At present, almost half of India's population live in unlettered darkness. Her literacy rate is now about 52 per cent. It becomes increasingly difficult to provide adequate educational resources to catch up with the nation's birth-rate. The supply of trained teachers, text books, school buildings and equipments is not adequate to meet the demands of the swelling army of school-going youngsters. The problem of providing primary education is so enormous that the adult literacy programme on a large scale cannot be effectively taken up at this stage. One of the paradoxes in the Indian literacy situation is that while the percentage of literacy has been increasing with each passing decade, the illiterates too have been increasing in number due to the abnormal increase in population.

Although India is, by and large, an agricultural country, agricultural production is markedly low in comparison with countries like Japan, not to speak of other countries like U.S.A. Canada, etc. Industrial production is fairly impressive and advances are being made in every sector of the economy through the developmental plans in the country. But the standard of living of an overwhelming majority of population continues to be below the poverty line. This is an indication that the improvement in production and the gain in national income are all diluted by the unprecedented increase in population. The total national income of India rose by about 40 per cent during the first two Five Year Plans, but the per capita income during the same period increased only by 19 per cent. However the real income and the consumption levels of the average Indian have not substantially improved. So, the basic economic problem in India is demographic.

Demographically India is moving so fast that despite all the progress being made, she remains economically almost static. It becomes well-nigh impossible for the country to make much headway in bringing about improvement in the fields of education, public health, sanitation, rural reconstruction, etc., due to the alarming increase of about sixteen million people each year. At this rate of population growth, India produces a population which is equivalent to One Australia every year. Even the law and order situation has deteriorated, people's mental peace is disturbed, their sense of discipline is lost and the entire value system seems to be degraded under the impact of enormous population growth. Today people are unable to move about in safety. Trains, buses and other modes of conveyance are overwhelmingly crowded and long distance travelling now becomes a nightmare.

The lofty principles of human rights which are often discussed at international and national forums are never observed in any area of day-to-day life. The malady lies perhaps with the lack of management and that is due to the tremendous increase of population and the consequent unusual increase in the demands of various services in all spheres of life. The existing medical, communication and other facilities are not adequate to meet the demands of the increasing population. The population of India has grown steadily during the current century except for a decrease in the decade 1911-21. The growth rate has been very high after 1951 and if this trend continues, India's population will be close to a billion by the turn of this century.

With the advance of urbanisation, the problem of slums is also raising its ugly head. About 30 per cent of the population in the metropolitan cities are estimated to be slum dwellers. The country's slum population is expected to touch 62 million by the year 2000 of which 32 million would be living in the metropolitan cities. By then about 87 million new dwelling units would be needed. Urbanisation is regarded as an indicator of progress. But in terms of the quality of life and social tensions arising from the growing slum dwellers being condemned to sub-human existence, it has indeed an appalling prospect. Actually, urbanisation in India is a voluntary process and cannot be stopped or reversed given the country's constitutional and legal framework. Even totalitarian countries like China have failed to check its growing urbanisation. Of course, an active birth control policy there has helped to control the problem. Thus, the growth of population in India is the direct result of the country's rapidly growing birth rate. Unless this basic problem is addressed, slum clearance and rehabilitation will be followed by bigger slums with resultant chaos and confusion.

The present trend of increase in population leads one to think of the gloomy prognosis by Robert Malthus. He opined that unless population was kept down to the level of the means of subsistence, the prospect of society was extremely bleak. He saw a natural tendency towards imbalance between the rates of growth of a population and its food supply. Therefore, he sounded a note of warning that if preventive checks were not applied to the ever increasing growth of population, nature would have its cruel ways of eliminating redundant population. Hence, the necessity arises to adopt various control measures to stave off the rapid population growth. It is all the more imperative for India to take immediate steps to hold in check the continuous growth of population and it may be possible by effectively implementing the family planning and population control programmes. The birth-rate may decline as a result of the improvement of the standard of living; but the hope of such improvements will be belied if there is a constant increase of population. There are, of course, different views on the question of the relation between the birth-rate and the standard of living. One school maintains that once the standard of living is raised, willy nilly the birth-rate will tend to fall because the people, having enjoyed the comforts of a higher standard of living, will like to retain it at any cost and as such will have preference for smaller families. According to this view, it is essential to increase overall agricultural and industrial production with a view to raising the per capita income of the people and with the improvement of their economic condition the birth-rate will automatically fall. The other view is that a community's low level of living cannot be raised unless the birth-rate is reduced because the new arrivals consume the increased quantum of output and the community remains with the same standard of living.

The increase in population including the working population does not ipso facto lead to proportional increase in production. The problems of unemployment and underemployment further worsen the situation. It is a fact that some thinly populated countries like Afghanistan are poor whereas such thickly populated countries as Belgium and the Netherlands are very rich with a high standard of living. This indicates that population is related to production. But production does not increase with the increase of population. In the present circumstances, it is difficult to significantly raise the standard of living in India unless the birth-rate is drastically slashed down. It is now amply realised that population can be controlled only by the reduction of the birth-rate and this goal can be achieved through the family planning programme. Any progress in this respect depends first on creating a sufficiently strong motivation in favour of family planning in the minds of the people and secondly on providing necessary advice and services based on acceptable, efficient, harmless and economic methods. The U.N. World Population Conference held in Bucharest in 1974 noted that parental motivation on the size of families is a key factor in the reduction of birth-rate.

The report of the 1961 Census brought out the explosive nature of the growth of population in India and the Government of India felt the urgent need for controlling it. Accordingly, the Third Five Year Plan considered the objective of stabilising the growth of population as part of the planned development. The Fourth Five Year Plan also gave considerable emphasis on the national family planning programme. In the successive Five Year Plans an increasing importance was attached to this programme by providing funds generously. Moreover, the Government of India adopted the National Population Policy in 1976 which envisaged a series of political, economic and social measures to promote family planning. The policy was, however, modified in 1977 to eliminate all forms of compulsion and coercion in the family planning programme embracing all aspects of family welfare including maternal and child health, nutrition, female education and women's rights. In accordance with this policy, all the methods were to be made available to the people and it was open to each family to decide about the method it would like to adopt. In spite of all these efforts, India's family planning programme has not made any significant progress. The fact is that the motivation approach is a long drawn-out process and it takes time to show any tangible result. For expeditious results, it is to be considered whether coercive methods should be adopted to put a brake on the escalating population growth.

Even in the hoary past, Plato in his '*Republic*' sought to formulate a theory of eugenic reform by establishing a relation between population increase and warfare. Aristotle also advocated a rigid control of marriage and a compulsory limitation on the family size based on property standards. Hamurabi's law in Babylon prescribed the penalty for induced abortion if the woman was injured. In India, the population pressure on scarce resources was felt long ago and varied institutional checks on the population growth were also introduced. The widespread observance of such practices as Sati, infanticide and prohibition against widow remarriage might be attributed to the ultimate aim of limiting the population growth. These were, of course, very cruel methods to prune the population growth and to bring about a balance between the size of the population and the resources available. Besides these, there are authentic views of different religions.

In the *Atharva Veda,* there are some references which indicate that abortion was known in the Vedic age. Kautilya's *Arthasastra* prescribes punishments for causing miscarriage by physical assault. The Parsi *Avesta* condemns abortion. Various Ayurvedic texts contain elaborate discussions on natural and induced abortion and treatment for preventing an abortion. Similarly, the Islamic texts contain varied approaches to the general issue of family planning by means of sterilisation and other devices. The Holy Quran contains several verses giving support to the concept of population control by adopting measures for planning a family. Various Muslim religious leaders in many countries of the world have also expressed their views in support of the family planning measures. Likewise, the code of Canon Law for the Christians does not specifically prohibit the adoption of birth control measures. Notwithstanding these views of different religions in favour of controlling family size, the prevalent attitude is, by and large, averse to the idea of family planning. Sterilisation as a mode of population control has not yet received wide popular acceptance.

In the past, abortion was regarded as an immoral act striking at the sanctity of life and this view was embodied in the Indian Penal Code, 1860. As a matter of fact, this view is widely supported even today by several segments of Indian society. The Government of India enacted the Medical Termination of Pregnancy Act in 1971 to facilitate the riddance of unwanted pregnancies. This Act allows elimination of an unwanted pregnancy of a married woman for the simple reason that a contraceptive device used by the couple failed to accomplish the desired purpose of limiting the family size. However, certain religious, social and political factors still affect the implementation of the Act.

In view of the present explosive demographic trend in India, the family planning programme should be implemented more effectively and vigorously. The infrastructure for implementing the programme should also be more meaningfully overhauled. The subject of population control is now saddled on the Ministry of Health which is already overburdened with a hundred of other pressing problems like prevention and control of disease; improvement of sanitation and hygiene, drug abuse control, etc. So there should be a separate Ministry of Population Control with a time bound programme of action. Mass education campaign also needs to be geared up in the rural and semi-urban areas. The traditional and cultural media like song and drama, folklore and puppet shows should be effectively used to motivate couples in the reproductive age-groups to adopt family planning.

Active involvement of village communities, especially women and private medical practitioners including nurses and mid-wives is essential for the success of the family planning programme. A study conducted by a U.S.-based non-governmental organisation, Centre for Development and Population Activities revealed that in some developing countries like Bangladesh, Sri Lanka, Indonesia, Egypt, Phillipines, Ecuador and Nigeria considerable success has been achieved in this respect through the adoption of a variety of community-based methods. It further pointed out that India could hardly make any substantial progress on the family planning front as the emphasis is given on the impersonal disbursal of contraceptives through governmental outlets only. Moreover, this country has relied heavily on the use of surgical contraception rather than the community-based methods. But in marked contrast to this practice in India, community-based distributors are engaged to supply contraceptives in the rural areas of Bangladesh and Sri Lanka. In Indonesia, private doctors and midwives have made significant contributions. Almost all Indonesian doctors are now participating in the programme. The study has also brought into focus some crucial factors responsible for success in these countries:

(1) Explicit and sustained political commitment, leadership and strategic management applied at all programme levels;

(2) access to a wide range of contraceptive methods provided through a variety of service delivery systems, especially the use of community-based distribution network;

(3) broader participation of private sector;

(4) a contraceptive logistics system to ensure availability;
(5) training to the programme staff at all levels;
(6) experiment and demonstration studies, and
(7) information, education and communication.

In addition to a strong political leadership and commitment, the local groups concentrating on research and dissemination of the family planning ideas should be strengthened. The local groups usually have a good public image and understanding of the local contexts. They are better equipped to analyse population dynamics and related issues at local levels. The results of such analyses can be conveniently disseminated to all concerned including opinion leaders of the community, programme managers, physicians, religious leaders and government functionaries.

THE PROBLEMS OF THE AGED

Old age and death are unavoidable and irreversible life processes. William Shakespeare aptly described the last phase of the seven stages of man:

> "Last of all,
> That ends this strange eventful history,
> Is second childishness and mere oblivion,
> Sans teeth, sans eyes, sans taste, sans everything."

About one fourth of a man's life is spent in growing up and preparing for active participation in society. Similarly, about one half is engaged in a variety of activities in an attempt to gain happiness and the final quarter of life is spent in a progressive process of reduced activity leading to physical decline followed by inevitable death. The process of decline during the last part of life becomes a problem not only for the person concerned, but also for the close relatives and the society as a whole. A sense of insecurity and helplessness prevails. Moreover, the loss of their status in the family, caste group and community becomes a source of utter frustration and maladjustment.

In ancient societies old people were widely respected. Among the ancient Herbrews, Greeks and Romans, those who were on the threshold of the last phase of their life cycles were believed to have mystical power, dominating wisdom and unquestionable authority. In India also, old age evoked deep respect and honour in the tradional society. In the joint family system a sort of gerontocracy prevailed. It was customary to obey the directions of the eldest member of the family. His decision was final in all matters. Even today, the elderly persons are respected and well looked after in the Indian joint families. They are considered to be the best source of social education, social service and social cohesion. Their experience and perceptive ideas are invaluable assets for the development of community. But, with the passage of time, the position is gradually undergoing a change. The process of industrialisation, urbanisation, social mobility, easy communication facilities and individualism is a predominant factor in transforming the traditional way of life in the community. Thus, the wind of change brought about by modernisation and technological advances has affected the traditional ties and earlier emotional links. The younger people migrate to urban areas leaving behind their congenial rural habitats. They are virtually thrown into a life of uncertainty and anonymity. Under such predicament, the old who stay behind, can not be taken care of nor do they have the same prestige and honour as they used to enjoy earlier.

With the increase of the total population, the number of the aged is also increasing in India as in other countries of the world. According to the UNESCO estimate, the number of the aged above 60 is likely to go up from 350 million in 1975 to 590 million in 2005. About half of them are in the developing countries. In the advanced countries like Norway, Sweden and Japan the proportion of the aged above 60 is 20 per cent. However, the percentage of the aged in other advanced countries in the West is in the neighbourhood of 14. In India, out of the total population of 685,184, 692 (Census, 1981), the aged, i.e., those who are above 60 years, form only about 6.3 per cent. The female aged out number the male aged. In fact, the population of the aged in India has been increasing constantly. In 1901, as the Census reveals, there were about 12 million people above the age of 60. In the next 50 years, i.e., in 1951, the population of the aged was 20 million. In the next 30 years from 1951 to 1981, the population of the aged rose to 43 million.

Now the population of the aged is about 48 million in India. On the basis of this calculation, it is expected that their population will exceed 67 million by the turn of this century. This

required to maintain his parents who are unable to maintain themselves. Similarly, section 20(3) of the Hindu Adoptions and Maintenance Act, 1956 also makes it obligatory on the part of a person to maintain his or her aged and infirm parents. Besides these legal provisions, the age-old practice in pursuance of the religious, cultural and social heritage of India is to take care of the aged in the family and the community and to enable them to lead a life of fulfilment and contentment. It is regarded as a moral duty of children to provide financial and physical security to their parents in old age. Children are, therefore, the eyes, ears, hands and feet to their aged parents.

As man grows older, every part of his body gradually wears out. In a developing country like India, poverty and malnutrition play a vital role in causing many diseases. Apart from malnutrition and diseases, the kind of life one leads, determines the pace of ageing. The elderly people who have suffered from protracted illness, higher burden of family responsibilities, constant worries and anxieties, excessive smoke and drink become older much earlier. However, many of the health problems and impairments that occur in old age, can be checked or delayed to a considerable extent, if proper preventive health care is taken well in time. It is, therefore, necessary to impart health education to people so that they may take timely preventive and curative steps for healthy lives in later years. The community should also be made aware of preventive, curative and rehabilitative needs of the old. There is no separate health service for the aged in our country. They have to make use of the general health care facilities available at the government hospitals and dispensaries. Private practitioners of various systems of medicine, medical services run by some voluntary agencies and in certain sectors insurance-based schemes like Employees State Insurance schemes, Central Government Health Scheme, Schemes for Railway Employees, Defence personnel, etc., also cater to the needs of the retired aged people.

However, it is necessary to have adequate geriatric clinical services within the existing general medical institutions to cope with the health problems of the aged. Courses in geriatric studies should be introduced in medical colleges so that physicians may be motivated and equipped with deeper knowledge on the subject. Medical camps and mobile medical care facilities are also essential for the old people. Old age is really not a disease. But the aged people are often vulnerable to long-term diseases like cardiovascular and cerebrovascular disease, mental derangement, cancer and pathological conditions affecting the locomotor system of hearing and vision. These diseases produce disabilities that make them dependent on the assistance of other people. However, these disabilities can be postponed or even eliminated by early detection and proper treatment.

Besides the above health care aspects, suitable living accommodation and congenial physical surroundings are necessary for healthy and socially useful life of the old people. It is a fact that housing has a great influence on the quality of life of any age-group. It is all the more important for the aged as most of their activities are confined to their dwelling places. A majority of the old people prefer to live near their relatives and friends to avoid loneliness and isolation. In some cases, group housing is suitable for facilities of social life, recreation and leisure. In general, housing for the aged should be adequate not only for their changed living patterns but also for the conditions of their declining health as usual in the later years of life. Those who have already retired from active service or those on the verge of retirement, should receive priority for allotment of houses and the cost of dwelling should also be subsidized for them. Those who cannot afford to buy houses may be given the facility on subsidised rents Development agencies, improvement trusts and housing boards should meet this objective.

A majority of the aged people suffer from economic hardships. Those who depend on agriculture for their livelihood in rural areas, do not have worthwhile schemes for economic security during their old age when morbidity and physical disabilities have full grip on them. Of late, the old age pension scheme has been introduced by the State Governments. But the quantum of such assistance is woefully meagre. However, the eligibility criteria for the old age pension differs from State to State. Most of the States have laid down 65 years as the minimum age for eligibility while in a few States the age limit is 60. Some States have prescribed a lower age limit for the females, widows and for persons suffering from physical or mental handicaps. The rate of pension ranges from Rs. 30 per month to Rs. 100 per month. Moreover, the coverage under the scheme is not uniform in all the States. This scheme has attracted attention of a number of committees and Study Groups.

The Study Group on Income and Wages, 1978 recognised the needs of the old people not covered by pensions and other benefits and suggested that there should be some standardization of the criteria adopted by different States for giving old age pension to the destitute aged. Similarly, the seventh Finance Commission, 1979 deliberated on the varying systems of payment of old age pension in different States and observed that it was desirable to have some uniformity in this regard. The Working Group constituted by the Economic Administration Reforms Commission, 1984 recommended that the Central Government should take a major initiative to promote a reformed and enlarged old age pension scheme and provide necessary financial support to the States for its implementation. The Committee on Petitions (Eighth Lok Sabha) also recommended a uniform rate of old age pension at Rs 150 per month. Moreover, the Sub-Committee of the Parliamentary Consultative Committee for the Ministry of Labour for Studying and Reporting on The Problems of Unorganised Workers in Agricultural sectors, 1988 has recommended that the age limit for eligibility for old age pension should, in no case, be over 60 years and in the case of females, it should be less than that of males.

It is also worth mentioning that voluntary organisations in India have been playing an important role in the care of the aged. They provide a wide range of services, viz., residential care, day care, geriatric care, medical and psychiatric care, recreation, financial assistance, counselling and guidance, etc. The scheme of homes for the aged caters to the needs of the destitute old people. The State Governments extend financial assistance to voluntary organisations for maintenance of these homes. At present, there are about 210 such homes in the country. These homes can not, however, provide necessary love, affection and emotional support required by the old people. The family is, therefore, the only place for them. The tradition of family bonds should be strengthened to solve many problems of the aged instead of proliferating homes for the aged. Governmental and voluntary organisations should establish social services to support the families where there are old people, especially those with low income.

Earlier, there was no specific welfare scheme for the aged at the national level. The Ministry of Welfare, Government of India provided grants-in-aid to voluntary organisations for rendering services to the aged since 1983-84. Recently, a new scheme under Central sector has been launched by the Ministry for the Welfare of the Aged. It is to be implemented through voluntary organisations for providing services like foster-care, day-care, old age homes, mobile medicare, etc. An amount of Rs. 10 crores* has been earmarked for the scheme during the current Five Year Plan. Voluntary Organisations should also take part in mobilising the services of the retired people and provide them with means and guidance so that they can contribute to the well-being of the community as a whole and the aged in paritcular. Spare time of the old people who are capable and willing may be put to use in community work such as adult literacy, welfare work among women, children and the handicapped, relief work, legal aid, etc. In Japan, more than 50,000 voluntary probation officers are mostly retired persons. They are imparted training to enable them to properly discharge their functions. Likewise, if some selected retired persons are imparted training in the care of the old and infirm, they can help in supplementing the efforts of the governmental and non-governmental organisations.

The problem of old age is gradually assuming considerable proportions. The number of maladujusted old people is constantly increasing. It has, therefore, emerged as an improtant social problem. There is need for a clear-cut national policy to effectively deal with this problem. A National Board for Care of the Aged may be set up on the lines of National Children's Board with a view to pursuing the National Policy on the Care and Welfare of the Aged. It may consist of representatives of concerned Ministries, eg., Health, Welfare, Finance, Law, Housing, etc. Moreover, professional experts in the fields of health, sociology, demography, economics and voluntary organisations may also be associated with the functions of the Board. This Board may promote, coordinate, monitor, evaluate and review various programmes and services for the care and welfare of the aged.

It is essential to create mass awareness of various problems of the aged amongst policy-makers, planners, administrators, medical and health experts, para-medical personnel and the population at large. In this connection it may be pointed out that research is an important activity in formulating, evaluating and implementing policies and programmes. This can be undertaken with

*Source: Annual Report 1992–93, Ministry of Welfare, Government of India.

the help of universities, research institutions and academicians of repute. The Ministry of Welfare, Government of India has already sponsored some new studies on ageing.* Valuable information available from such nation-wide researches and surveys on these problems may be circulated extensively in the country and seminars, workshops, conferences, etc., may also be organised to focus public attention on the newly emerging geriatric problems. Voluntary organisations especially Indian Medical Association should take the lead in publishing a useful material to highlight various geriatric problems and their possible solution in keeping with the existing national resources at regular intervals.

SOCIAL CHANGE AND DEVELOPMENT

Social change is an important phenomenon in the history of mankind. In every living society there is always some movement for change. Minor changes may not be perceptible or explicitly visible. There may be peaceful adaptation to new ideas without changing tradition and way of life. As such, there may not be any apparent social change. Real social change occurs when there is large-scale alterations in the social structure, old value system and established institutions. In the process of such a change, indiscipline, chaos, confusion and uncertainty prevail. As human nature is aganist any violent radical change in the existing set-up, any large-scale social change is unlikely to be accepted immediately. In India, this problem is all the more acute. In view of her vast size and multiplicity of cultures and social ethos, it becomes difficult to bring about any social change at the national level. Social change has, of course, occurred due to the advent of the great religious leaders—like Gautama Buddha, Sankaracharya, Guru Nanak and others in this country.

In the realm of ideas also, changes were triggered off by the charismatic personalities like Swami Vivekananda, Swami Dayananda and Ramana Maharshi. Swami Vivekananada's call to the nation, particularly the youth of the country in the words of *Upanishada* "Arise, awake and stop not till the goal is reached" still vibrates in the air and enthuses generations to come. While elucidating the true meaning of religion, he opined "first of all, our

*Source: Annual Report, 1992–93, Ministry of Welfare, Government of India.

young men must be strong. Religion will come afterwards. Be strong, my young friends. You will be nearer to heaven through football than through the study of Gita. You will understand the Gita better with your biceps, your muscles a little stronger." Similarly, Swami Dayananda preached vedic religion. His watch-word was 'Back to the Vedas.' He was against idol-worship and taught people to have faith in one God. He condemned the caste-system, useless religious sacrifices, rituals and superstitions. He also fought against untouchability and caste restrictions. In fact, the entire social structure underwent a change in the process of absorbing the new ideas.

In India, the process of change began in the 19th century and accelerated during the current century. The first half of this century was dominated by Mahatma Gandhi and the national freedom movement. When India won her independence, various laudable measures, namly, democracy, socialistic pattern of society and planned economy were undertaken. Development of science, technology and communications have also ushered in a new era of change in the country. The use of science and technology in everyday life is not only reducing the drudgery of life but also levelling down distinctions and breaking the tyranny of rituals and traditional customs. Equality before law, the increasing emphasis on social justice, progressive social and welfare legislation are all combining to strengthen social change towards a less hierarchical, more democratic and less unequal society.

Changes are also taking place in the family sphere. The traditional joint family system which provided security to its members is gradually being abolished and the nuclear family is coming into existence. The age of marriage is rising and the baneful effects of child marriage is now widely felt by the people. Now-a-days, inter-caste, inter-sub-caste, inter-lingual, inter-regional and inter-religious marriages are on the increase. This is a congenial trend which may lead to national integration. The traditional pattern of behaviour is now seldom visible. Relations between parents and children, husbands and wives are undergoing changes. Women have now more freedom and occupy a better position in respect of social and economic conditions. As a matter of fact, society cannot thrive unless women's position is improved. In this connection, the great seer Swami Vivekananda observed that the welfare of the world can be ensured only when the condition of women is improved. Since independence, various legislative as well as administrative measures have been taken to elevate the status of women in society. The Goverment of India had set up a committee on status of women in the seventies to study in detail the conditions in respect of women and to suggest measures for the improvement of their conditions. The latest action of the Government of India to appoint a Women's Commission is indeed a step in the right direction.

There is a trend for improving the social status and the opportunity and advancement of the under-privileged and traditionally backward sections of the society. In other words, there is an overall trend in social change towards freeing the individual from traditional restraints, and restructuring human relations in terms of functions and powers in place of heredity and traditional authority. The Brahmins being the highest caste in the Hindu hierarchy were given traditional authority and defferential position by the Hindu law-givers. Now there is a tendency to relegate them from their erstwhile high pedestal either by acquiring their qualities or by despising them. The Brahmins also respond to the wind of social change by accepting the fait accompli. In so doing, the Brahmins have become instrumental in bringing about the desired social change and modernisation. In consequence of such social changes, the process of sanskritisation has taken place. By this process, the lower castes, tribes or other backward groups of people start imitating the higher castes and adopt their customs, rituals, beliefs, ideology and style of life.

In the past, various low-caste Hindus were under the yoke of caste hierarchy. Now they have sought to get out of the caste tyranny in a bid to improve their social status. Thus, a large number of lower caste Hindus have been converted into non-Hindu faiths. Some of these people have formed new groups within the Hindu fold that owes no allegiance to the Hindu higher castes. The examples of Lingayats in the South and the Vaisnavas in the East may be cited in this connection. In some places Harijans were also converted to Buddhism with a view to getting released from the bonds of Hindu caste hierarchy. There were also movements spearheaded by some groups like D.M.K. in Tamil Nadu for moving up the caste ladder to improve their socio-economic status. Poet Rabindranath Tagore could visualise this situation of social cleavage long ago and gave a clarion call to the nation:

"Come ye, who are shunned and isolated,
Wipe out all dishonour,
Come to the crowning of the mother,
Fill the sacred bowl with water
That is sanctified by the touch of all."

The age-old rigidity of caste system is now on the decline. The outlook of the people has definitely undergone a change. Of course, the incidence and the tempo of such social changes are much higher in towns and cities than in villages. So, urbanisation is held to be one of the causes of social change. There has been a phenomenal increase in the urban population which has consequently led to a number of problems like break-up of traditional joint family system, lack of social control, anonymity, culture conflict, over-crowded conditions, etc.

The population in India is increasing by leaps and bounds. According to the census of 1981, India has a population of 685,184,692. But the latest statistics indicate that it has grown to 843,930,861 of which about 23.8% is urban. As a result of the large-scale migration of people from the rural areas to the urban areas, the original community feelings are gradually waning and people have become extremely self-centred. Civic sense or a desire for the weal of others appears to be absent. This tendency has, of late, become very acute. Very few people now think in terms of others. The freedom struggle in the past generated a tremendous national feeling among the Indian masses; but that feeling which had brought all of them together cutting across the barriers of religions, castes or creeds, that national feeling—that feeling of unity and devotion is almost extinct now. A divisive force has now overtaken the entire country. Every section of people through the length and breadth of the country wants their separate entity. The evils of regionalism and linguism are raising their ugly heads. What is worse, religious revivalism and a new form of egalitarianism are also manifesting themselves. This trend, unless taken care of with utmost sagacity at the initial stage, will spell disaster for the nation as a whole.

Secularism is a new phenomenon which seeks to reject theocracy and guarantee equality to all citizens. It gives importance to political, economic, artistic and other aspects of social life, relegating the necessity of rituals and festivals associated with different religions. This has ultimately led to the loosening of inhibitive ties among followers of different faiths and undermined the hold of rituals and religious occasions in social life, which earlier provided a congenial atmosphere for getting together at the community level. In consequence, religions and rituals are no longer an affair of public life. These have become entirely private affairs of individuals. Now secularism is slackening the bonds of inter-religious barriers and promoting new ways of life for people getting together in clubs, gymnasia, restaurants, meetings, seminars and conferences in pursuit of multifarious common objectives. This trend may be a good portent if it leads to a casteless humanism and catholicity.

Westernization is also another factor which has considerably influenced the Indian society. It is a process of social change having far-reaching consequences in India. This change is not only confined to urban areas but to semi-urban and rural areas as well. There is a wide-spread craze for the English language, clothing habits, food habits, which are gradually being absorbed in the Indian way of life. The Swadeshi movement and the preachings of the patriotic and religious leaders and social reformers like Swami Vivekananda, Swami Dayananda, Srichaitanya, Mahatma Gandhi and Rabindranath Tagore did, to some extent, stem.... the tide of westernization in the country; but it was only a temporary phase. What is more surprising is that the drift towards westernization has increased after independence. This process gathered momentum due to industrialization, unabated urbanization and accelerating technological developments. Moreover, the western way of life of political leaders and public men has also influenced people to a large extent.

Nationalism is a prominent factor in bringing about social change. It helps in shaking off parochialism, narrowness and other concomitant evils. In India, it has set in a trend for breaking down caste-barriers and creating a multi-lingual casteless society which has no conformity with the traditional way of life. This trend has reduced the hold of traditional way of life and strengthened the move towards modernity. The movement for democracy, elections and socialism are all an offshoot of nationalism. The popular upsurge in Nepal a few years ago may be cited as an example. The ultimate objective of all such movements is to do away with the traditional hierarchical structure and to promote the desire for human dignity. The aim is also to give the underprivileged a feeling of importance and a sense of belonging, thus making for a less unequal society with access to a variety of opportunities. This kind of social change is leading us near to the frame-work of western democratic societies. Moreover, the introduction of new tools, gadgets, electricity, gas, pipewater, underground drainage, rail transport and airways has brought about a revolutionary change in the Indian social milieu.

The problems created by rapid population growth and tardy social and economic development will be gradually acute. It will be a formidable task for the government to provide essential services to the teeming population in the years to come. It will be difficult even to secure health and employment. It is, therefore, imperative to reduce the rate of population growth as a necessary corollary to social and economic development. Steps should also be taken to improve technology. This will, of course, call for investment, training, orientation, social reorganisation and restructuring the distributive system. What is more, social reorganisation and appropriate technological progress should proceed simultaneously with the reduction in population.

The partition of India in 1947 led to a massive movement of refugees between India and Pakistan. The major impact of this large-scale migration of refugees was on the cities of India. But the Indian cities did not have the physical and economic infrastructure to cope up with the demands made by the uprooted humanity for their residential land, housing, water supply, sewerage, transport and so on. Moreover, an unending migration of rural people to urban areas has made the problems all the more alarming. The increasing influx of people in the cities has led to the unplanned expansion of urban areas and growth of slums with all their accompanying evils. Gandhiji, therefore, looked upon urbanisation as an evil as it was totally divorced from the rural way of life rooted in nature. He observed, "I regard the growth of the cities as an evil thing, unfortunate for mankind and the world.... The blood of the villages is the current with which the edifice of the cities is built." He further expressed, "I want the blood that is inflating the arteries of the cities to run once again in the blood vessels of the villages; I do not want to depopulate the cities and send the city folk back to villages. All I want is that they should readjust their lives so as to cease to sponge upon the poor village folk and make to the latter what reparation is possible, even at this late hour, by helping to resuscitate their ruined economy." This approach of Mahatma Gandhi could be adopted as a viable alternative to the existing trend of continuous migration of rural people to urban areas. Agriculture and agro-industries can be developed on scientific lines to ameliorate the deplorable conditions of the rural masses. Further, a rational approach to the problem of unemployment is necessary in both rural and urban areas based on generating mobility of labour in a planned manner without distubring the congenial social conditions in villages.

However, according to poet Rabindranath Tagore, the problem of rural reconstruction required not only the removal of poverty, but also providing joy to the life of the villagers. With this end in view, he established Sriniketan, the institute of Rural Reconstruction in 1921 along with Vishwa Bharati at Santiniketan. The aims of this Institute were: (1) to study the problems of the villagers and provide solutions to them, (2) to develop their resources and credit system, (3) to teach them better methods of growing crops and vegetables and of keeping the live-stock and (4) to encourage them to learn and practise arts and crafts and to convince them of the benefits of associated life, mutual help and common endeavour. With the similar objective Gopal Krishna Gokhale organised the Servants of India Society in 1905 and established a number of centres for carrying out rural reconstruction work. Its activities included child welfare, poultry rearing, introduction of improved agricultural method, cottage industries and imparting training in agriculture, animal husbandry and textile wearing, etc. Such activities were also carried on by various Christian missionaries.

After independence, rural welfare programmes were undertaken by the government to improve the conditions of the rural masses. The community projects and the national extension service schemes were initiated under the Five Year Plans. Through these schemes, it was sought to start a process of transformation of the social and economic life of villagers. In spite of all these efforts, there is a lack of adequate progress in one important area, i.e., education. In fact, education is a predominant factor in generating a sense of social responsibility, discipline and lofty ideas among the people. One reason which hampers the progress of education in villages is that there is no wide-spread demand for it among the poor and the weaker sections of the people. As they are uneducated and illiterate, they do not see any advantagve in being literate by attending schools. This attitude might have been reinforced by the general irrelevance of the school programme to the future life of their children. Some of the villagers regard education as an undesirable activity which alienates children from the work and life to which they are destined. Thus, poverty is the important reason for such feelings among the rural people. Most of the children who do not go to school at all and those who drop out of schools, come from families which live below the poverty line. So, poverty has been a handicap for the spread of education. Despite wide literacy campaigns and extension of educational facilities, the progress in this sphere is very tardy. All efforts to ameliorate the conditions of the people will be in vain unless they are well-educated and well-cared for.

The Constitution of India provides for free, universal and compulsory education for children upto the age of 14 years. But this objective could not so far be achieved due to the backwardness of certain areas and certain sections of the people. Along with the extension of educational facilities, the pattern of education should also be changed so as to enable children to learn some crafts as well. Moreover, it is essential in rural areas to persuade all parents and guardians to send their children to schools. If the school holidays in rural areas are so planned as to coincide with the harvesting and sowing seasons, parents may not have any objection to their children's continuing studies.

Distance often prevents parents from sending their children to schools. Hence, schools should be conveniently located so that every child may easily take advantage of the facility. Many superstitious and myopic ideas still persist among the rural folk due to their colossal ignorance. Although a massive social change is now afoot in India, it appears it will take time to bring about a desirable change in the age-old rural social structure.

BIBLIOGRAPHY

Abadinsky, Howard: Probation and Parole: Theory and Practice, Englewood Cliffs, New Jersey, Prentice-Hall, Inc., 1977.

Advani, N.H.: Perspective on Adult Crime and Corrections, New Delhi, Abhinav Publications, 1978.

Adams, Thomas F.: Criminal Justice Readings, California, Good Year Publicity. Co., 1972.

Ahuja, Ram: Female Offenders in India, Meerut, Meenakshi Prakashan, 1969.

Ahuja, Ram: Crime Against Women, Jaipur, Rawat Publication, 1987.

Ancel, Marc: Social Defence, London, Routledge & Kegan Paul, 1965.

Attar, A.D.: Juvenile Delinquency—A comparative Study, Bombay, Popular Prakashan, 1962.

Barnes, E.H. & Teeters, N.K.: New Horizons in Criminology, Virginia, Prentice-Hall, Inc., 1966.

Bean, Philip: Rehabilitation and Deviance, London, Routledge & Kegan Paul, 1976.

Bender, David L.: Crime and Criminals: Opposing Viewpoints, Minnesota, Greenhaven Press, 1977.

Bergler, Edwund: The Psychology of Gambling, New York, Hill and Wang, 1943.

Bhattacharya, B.K.: Juvenile Delinquency and Borstals, Calcutta, S.C. Sarkar and Sons Private Ltd., 1962.

Bhattacharyya, S.K.: Social Defence—An Indian Perspective, Delhi, Manas Publications, 1985.

Bhattacharyya, S.K.: Prison and Probation—A Comparative Study on the Economic Aspects, Social Defence Journal, Vol IV, No. 4, 1968.

Bhattacharyya, S.K.: Probation Services: Obstacles in the Way of Development in India, Social Defence Journal, Vol V, No. 17, 1969.

Bhattacharyya, S.K.: Origin and Development of Probation, Journal of Correctional Work, No. 24, 1978.

Bhattacharyya, S.K.: Prevention of Begging, Social Defence Journal, Vol. X, No. 39, 1975.

Bhattacharyya, S.K.: Juvenile Justice System in India, Journal of the Indian Law Institute, Vol. 23, No. 4, 1982.

Bhattacharyya, S.K.: Trends in Crime and Corrections, Social Defence Journal, Vol. VI, No. 21, July 1970.

Bhattacharyya, S.K.: Juvenile Delinquents and the Law, Indian Journal of Criminology, Vol. 7, No. 2, July 1979.

Bhattacharyya, S.K.: Juvenile Delinquency and Development of Treatment Programmes, Social Health Journal, Vol. XIII, No. 1, 1975.

Bhattacharyya, S.K. Juvenile Delinquency—Its Prevention and Cure, Social Defence Journal, Vol. XI, No. 44, April, 1976.

Bhattacharyya, S.K.: Probation System in India—An Appraisal, Delhi, Manas Publications, 1987.

Bottomley, A.K.: Decisions in Penal Process, London, Martin Robertson & Co., 1973.

Brij Mohan: India's Social Problems, Allahabad, International Publications, 1972.

Briggs, Dennie: In place of Prison, London, Temple Smith Ltd., 1975.

Brody, S.R.: The Effectiveness of Sentencing—A Review of Literature, London, Her Majesty's Stationery Office, 1976.

Burkhart, Kartheryn Watterson: Women in Prison, New York, Doubleday, 1973.

Carney, Louis P.: Corrections and the Community, Englewood Cliffs, New Jersey, Prentice-Hall, Inc., 1977.

Chandra, Sushil: Sociology of Deviation in India, Bombay, Asia Publishing House, 1967.

Chohan, B.R.: Practice and Programmes in Juvenile Correction, Bombay, David Sassoon Industrial School, 1977.

Cohen, John: Substantive Probability, Scientific American 197:128-138, 1957.

Consul, S.C. : Probation of Offenders Acts and Rules (Central and States), Allahabad, Law Book Company, 1980.

Clatt, M.H.: Drugs, Society and Man—A guide to Addiction and Treatment, Lancaster, England, Medical and Technical Publishing Co., 1974.

Claridge, Gardon: Drugs and Human Behaviour, London, Penguin Press, 1970.

Clinard, Marshall B.: The Sociology of Deviant Behaviour (Rev. ed.), New York, Holt, Rinehart and Winston, Inc., 1963.

Das, S.: Crime and Punishment in Ancient India, New Delhi, Abhinav Publications, 1978.

Datar, R.N.: Prison as a Social System, Bombay, Popular Prakashan, 1978.

Desai, Neera and Patel, Vibhuti: Indian Women: Change and Challenge in the International Decade 1975–85, Bombay, Popular Prakashan, 1985.

Dewan, Vijay Kumar: Laws Relating to Terrorists, Delhi, Capital Law House, 1992.

Dholakia, R.P. & Rao, Narayana K.(Edt): Terrorism and International Law, New Delhi, Indian Society of International Law, 1988.

Durkheim, E.: The Rules of the Sociological Methods, New York, The Free Press, 1964.

Durkheim, E.: Crime as a Normal Phenomenon, New York, The Free Press, 1964.

Elliot, M.A.: Crime in Modern Society, New York, Harper, 1952.

Elliot M.A. & Merril, F.E.: Social Disorganisation, New York, Harper and Brothers, 1950.

Erikson, E.H.: Youth and Crisis, Delhi, Oxford University Press, 1968.

Frankin, David: The Strategy of Terrorism, Foreign Affairs, July, 1975, pp 683–698.

Ganguly, B.N.: Social Development: Essays in Honour of Durgabai Deshmukh, New Delhi, Sterling Publishers, 1977.

Ghurye, G.S.: Social Tensions in India, Bombay, Popular Prakashan Ltd., 1968.

Gibbons, Don C.: Society, Crime and Criminal Careers: An Introduction to Criminology, 3rd. Ed., New Jersey, Prentice-Hall, 1977.

Gillin, J.L.: Criminology and Penology, 3rd, Ed., London, D. Appleton-Century & Co., 1945.

Glaser, Daniel: Crime in Our Changing Society, New York, Halt, Reinehart and Winston, 1978.

Glover, Edward: Roots of Crime, London, Image Publications Co., 1960.

Gore, M.S.: Urbanization and Family Change, Bombay, Popular Prakashan, 1968.

Gupta, Giri Raj: Main Currents in Indian Sociology (Vol. IV), New Delhi, Vikas Publishing House Pvt. Ltd., 1979.

Gupta, J.L.: Challenges to the Fair Sex, Delhi, Gian Publishing House, 1988.

Hartjen, Clayton A.: Crime and Criminalisation, 2nd Ed., New York, Robert E. Krieger Publication Co. 1978.

Healey, W. and Bronner, A.F.: New Lights on Delinquency and its Treatment, Yale, Yale University Press, 1936.

Hendrickson, R.C.: Youth in Danger, New York, Harcourt Bruce, 1956.

Hyams, Edward: Terrorists and Terrorism, London, J.M. Dent,1975.

Jack, H.A.: Terrorism: Another U.N. Failure, America, October 20, 1973, pp 283–285.

Johnson, Elmer Hubert: Crime, Correction and Society: An Introduction to Criminology, London, Dossey Press, Homewood, 1978.

Khanna, Cirija and Mariamma A. Varghese: Indian Women Today, New Delhi, Vikas Publishing House, 1978.

Korn, Richard R. & McCorkle, Lloyd W.: Criminology and Penalogy, New York, Rinehart and Winston, 1959.

Lamert, E.M.: Social Pathology, New York, McGraw Hill, 1951.

Livingston, Jay: "Compulsive Gamblers: A Culture of Losers", Psychology Today, March, 1974

Madan, G.R.: Indian Social Problems, Vol I (2nd. Ed.), Bombay, Allied Publishers, 1969.

McCord, W. and McCord, J.: Origins of Crime, New York, Columbia University Press, 1959.

Ministry of Social Welfare, Govt. Of India: India—Country Paper at The Sixth United Nations Congress on the Prevention of Crime and the Treatment of Offenders, New Delhi, 1980.

Ministry of Social Welfare, Govt. Of India: Report of the Indian Delegation to the Sixth United Nations Congress on the Prevention of Crime and the Treatment of Offenders, New Delhi, 1980.

Mukherjee, Ram Krishna: Diagnosing Social Change, Delhi, Allied Publishers, 1979.

Norman Imlah: Drugs in Modern Society, London, Geoffrey Chaphan, 1970.

Pal, B.K.: Problems and Concerns of Indian Women, New Delhi, ABC Publishing House, 1987.

Panakal, J.J.: Court and Probation, Social Defence, Vol. V., No. 24, 1971.

Peterson, Virgil W: Gambling—Should It Be Legalized? Journal of Criminal Law and Criminology 40:259-329, Chicago Crime Commission, (1945) 1949.

Punekar, S.D. and Rao, Kamla: A Study of Prostitutes in Bombay, Bombay, Lalvani Publishing House, 1962.

Quinney, Richard: Problem of Crime: A Critical Introduction to Criminology, 2nd, Ed., New York, Harper and Row Publishers.

Radzinowicz, L. and Wolfgang, M.E.: Crime and Justice (Revised Ed.), New York, Basic Book Inc. Publishers, 1977.

Ramakrishna, P.V.: A Treatise on Anti-Corruption Law in India, Hyderabad, The Golconda Publications Ltd., 1969.

Rani Billimoria: Female Criminality, Delhi, Eastern Book Company, 1987.

Reckless, W.C.: Criminal Behaviours, New York, McGraw Hill, 1967.

Reckless, W.C.: Jail Administration In India, New York, United Nations Technical Assistance Programme, 1953.

Savitz, L.: Dilemma in Criminology, Virginia, Prentice-Hall, 1976.

Saksena, N.S.: Terrorism—History and Facets in the World and in India, New Delhi, Abhinav Publications, 1985.

Shah, Jyotsna H.: Studies in Criminology: Probation Services in India, Bombay, N.M. Tripathi, 1973.

Siddique, A.: Criminology: Problems & Perspectives, Lucknow, Eastern Book Co., 1962.

Smart, Carol: Women, Crime and Criminology, London Routledge and Kegan Paul, 1976.

Srivastava, T.N.: Women and the Law, New Delhi, Publishing House, 1985.

Sutherland, E.H. and Cressey, D: Principles of Criminology, Philadelphia. J.P. Lippincott, 1960.

Srivastava, S.P.: Public Participation in Social Defence, New Delhi, D.K. Publishers' Distributors, 1981.

Sinha, Raghuvir: Social Change in Indian Society, Delhi, Concept, 1979.

Taft, D.R.: Criminology, New York, Macmillan, 1956.

Tennebum, F.: Crime and Community, New York, Columbia, 1957.

Vasudeva, P.: Social Change, New Delhi, Sterling Pubiishers, 1967.

Wines, Frederick H.: Punishment and Reformation, New York, Thomas Y. Crowell & Co., 1919.

Zuckerman, Marvin: "The Search for High Sensation", Psychology Today, Febuary, 1978.

Report of the Indian Jails Committee, 1919–20.

Report of the All India Jail Manual Committee, 1957–59.

Report of the All India Committee on Jail Reforms, 1980–83.

Report of the National Expert Committee on Women Prisoners, 1986–87.